POINTS OF INTERSECTION

POINTS OF INTERSECTION

Meeting Paul Bowles, Allen Ginsberg, Brion Gysin, Robert Graves, Pauline Réage, and others

GREGORY STEPHENSON

EYECORNER PRESS

POINTS OF INTERSECTION:
Meeting Paul Bowles, Allen Ginsberg, Brion Gysin, Robert Graves, Pauline Réage, and others

Published by EYECORNER PRESS
August 2018, Thy, Denmark

ISBN: 978-87-92633-40-8

Cover design and layout: Camelia Elias
Editorial consultant: Bent Sørensen

All photographs by Birgit Stephenson

Grateful acknowledgement is made to the editors of magazines in which the essays in this volume have previously appeared: *Eclectica, Empty Mirror, Exquisite Corpse, Rain Taxi Review of Books, The Literary Review.*

Printed in the UK and US

ONCE MORE,
FOR BIRGIT

Also by Gregory Stephenson

Exiled Angel: A Study of the Work of Gregory Corso (1989)

The Daybreak Boys: Essays on the Literature of the Beat Generation (1990)

Out of the Night and into the Dream: A Study of the Fiction of J.G. Ballard (1991)

Comic Inferno: A Study of the Fiction of Robert Sheckley (1997)

Understanding Robert Stone (2002)

Pilgrims to Elsewhere: Reflections on Writings by Jack Kerouac, Allen Ginsberg, Gregory Corso, Bob Kaufman & Others (2013)

Contents

Introduction
A. Robert Lee

The art of discursive writing can get it in the neck from both ends.

To those who opt for literary high seriousness it can smack of mere passing observation, play it as it lays jottings. To the hardcore journalist it can seem to eschew the 5 Ws of conventional reportage (who, what, when, where, why).

But mid-way lies another register – keen-eyed, savvy, more ruminative. And given in duly engaging measure.

Throughout *Intersections* Gregory Stephenson pitches his tent just there.

It has to be a treat to follow the riffs and swerves of this collection. The first-person encounters with place, author, text and culture carry a welcome accessibility and rarely more so than when Stephenson writes at his most idiosyncratically observant. Surprises lie concealed. Riffs tease even as they catch the attention.

Not least of the factors in play in this regard lies in the persona of the author himself. Here is the longtime American expatriate from the open-space southwest of Arizona set down by choice and marriage within the peninsular north of Denmark. But the command of Danish acquired over the years has anything but inhibited his interest in the weighted history of Europe beyond the borders of Scandinavia. Quite the contrary.

The upshot amounts to a kind of literal and literary wall-panel, a roster of creative nonfiction drawn from life and enriched with bandwidths of international literature, painting, film, and never least, popular culture.

Copenhagen, Stephenson's adopted city of lost and found gloves in his own winning trope, provides the symptomatic opening flourish. This is the capital under Kirkegaard's statued gaze, stalked by the ghosts of a Gauguin, Céline or Isherwood, and affording the author a meeting with James Joyce's aged one-time teacher of Danish. The author's gaze readily alights on dark backstreets as much as the Danish parliament building, on the imposing Holberg chestnut tree (with a nice thread on the author for whom it is named) and his own rackety small flat, temporary manual jobs and thrift shop clothes-buying. A step back to the Vietnam years takes the un-blinkered view that many of the US "deserters" were in fact small-time crooks, with a notable portrait of the miscreant Greek American Philip Tsirakides whose dark Mediterranean skin regularly made him the butt of anti-black prejudice. Nostalgia is given free rein in Stephenson's listening amid airwave static to American sports and jazz broadcasts and in his editorship of the small but impressive literary journal *Pearl*. The knack throughout is to have knotted these facets of Copenhagen life, his own included, into one. The piece sets just the right temperature for *Intersections* as a whole.

In each of the contributions that follow the same attentiveness, and accompanying ease of manner, equally holds.

The Paul Bowles piece gives actuality both to Bowles himself, along with the great Moroccan storyteller trio of Mohamed Choukri, Larby Layachi, and Mohhamed Mrabet, and to Tangier as Maghreb arts outpost and city. Brion Gysin in physical decline but still a force for avant-garde composition gets full sympathetic attention. Robert Graves, doyen of the White Goddess and Mallorca, is captured in both his at-home domesticity and poet's quirk. Some nimble detective footwork comes into play for the essay on Pauline Réage/Dominique Auby and the hinterland to her *L'Histoire d'O* erotica. It does again in the portrait of Berthe Cleyrergue, one-time housekeeper to the renowned lesbian and greatly wealthy American expatriate and Paris *salonière* Nathalie Clifford Barney. Maurice Girodias, begetter of the Olympia Press, receives one of Stephenson's liveliest engravings as a mixture of publishing genius and rogue. Late night talk in Dieppe with the polyglot American writer-poet and painting *connoisseur* Eduard Roditi, accompaniment of Ginsberg and Orlovsky on their Copenhagen visit, and a personal retrospect on Arizona to Denmark "exile" (if such it really has been), each carry their own respective lights.

Gregory Stephenson is not about writing full-on cultural or literary critique. His aim is altogether more sly, the deftly surreptitious contemplations of the long-stay New to Old World visitor.

Non-Danish speakers like myself have good reason to say *Tusind Tak.*

Bios Xenikon Blues [I]

In winter the city is strewn with lost gloves. They lie on sidewalks and in the streets, flattened and forlorn. The blunt brown gloves of men and the slender-fingered black gloves of women, and saddest of all, the striped and brightly colored, wool-knit gloves of children.

Passing the statue of Søren Kierkegaard on my way into the Royal Library, I salute as always. He smiles dreamily under a dunce cap of snow. Kirkegaard is still very much a presence in Copenhagen (more especially on winter days.) You can visit his grave in Assistens Churchyard (his name means churchyard in Danish), read his letters and touch his furniture in a museum, drink beer in an old café that he once frequented. Heritage plaques mark the places of his birth and death. I see Danes reading his books on trains and in cafés and parks. I once worked here with two thin, timorous twins whom others had nicknamed "Angst" and "Bæven," (that is, "Fear" and "Trembling.") I particularly groove on the way in which Kirkegaard (like Hamlet before him) situates melancholy at the center of the human condition, calling it his "intimate confidante" and "faithful mistress."

Other famous ghosts in the streets of the city are those of Paul Gauguin, James Joyce, Louis Ferdinand Céline, Christopher Isherwood, Donald Barthelme and Robert McAlmon, all of whom lived here for a time. Gauguin was married to a Danish woman, and worked in Copenhagen as a tarpaulin salesman, before abandoning his wife and five children and moving to Tahiti. Enduring evidence of his having lived here includes family graves in Garnison's churchyard, paintings and sculptures in Copenhagen art museums, and living descendents, one of whom is a

Danish rock musician. Isherwood lived here in the 1930s with his German boyfriend. Céline, fearing prosecution as a Nazi collaborator, fled
from Germany to Copenhagen with his wife and cat, aboard the last
Swedish Red Cross train just days before the German surrender.

Arrested and imprisoned by Danish authorities, Céline wrote a fic-
tionalized memoir, *Féerie pour une autre* fois (*Fable for Another Time*),
in pencil in his prison cell, with passages detailing prison life in Vestre
Fængsel. Céline's experiences in Denmark are also treated by him in his
posthumously published hallucinatory novel, *Rigodon* (1969). Joyce who
could read and speak Danish fluently, concluded that Danish was "a
weeping language and the Danes a nation of weepers, of wild men with
soft voices." A delightful result of Joyce's sojourn in Copenhagen is the
children's story he wrote in a letter to his grandson, Stephen James Joyce,
titled *The Cats of Copenhagen.* And there are, of course, a number of
Danish words in *Finnegans Wake.*

On two occasions I met and spoke with Max Pedersen, who while
living in Paris during the late 1920s tutored Joyce in Danish. A frail, thin
old man, he remembered Joyce with fondness and sympathy, recalling
Joyce's fragile, slightly shabby appearance and weak eyes, referring to
him still as "that poor boy." Pedersen recalled how Joyce proposed that
they use passages from his own works for translation into Danish, and
use the Bible and Danish psalms for translation into English. Joyce, he
said, was quick to understand the nuances of Danish words, a serious and
very apt pupil despite having to use a magnifying glass in order to read.

I noted that Max Pedersen's personal copy of Joyce's *Dubliners* was
a worn, rubbed, dark green leatherette Modern Library edition from the
1920s, a volume contemporary with the time when they knew each other
in Paris. "That poor boy," he said again, in the eye of memory seeing
Joyce still, "he was nearly blind." And I (so strangely) seeing before me
an old man who had once seen James Joyce.

I have twice stood studying the red brick building at Classensgade 65 where Christopher Isherwood and his 19 year old German boyfriend, Heinz, lived from the autumn of 1934 to the spring of 1935. (Isherwood later recalled how "when icy rain or snow gusts drove down the Classensgade," he felt "the awful melancholia of the North"). I often wondered whether Isherwood had left behind him in Copenhagen any trace of his sojourn in the city. One frozen, snowy January afternoon, browsing in Bogormen, a modest cellar book shop run by ex-featherweight boxer and retired waiter Leon Sørensen, I found on a shelf there a copy of Isherwood's novel, *The Last of Mr. Norris* (N.Y. 1935). On the end paper of the book was a signed inscription: "To Fru Bækgaard, With much gratitude for all her kindness and hospitality to the author, Christopher Isherwood. May 1935."

The penciled price for this precious artifact was the equivalent of less than five dollars. Leon was always very kind to me, we often chatted about the great prizefighters and famous bouts of the past. I told him the Isherwood book was worth a good deal more than the price he was asking, but he generously insisted that I should have it anyway. "Old Mrs. Bækgaard," he told me, whose book it had been, had lived just around the corner. She had only recently died and he had bought a box of her books. Inside the covers of other Isherwood titles that Leon had bought (and that I then bought from him) Fru Bækgaard had written her name: Ellen Bækgaard.

I believe this must be the same Ellen Bækgaard (a committee member of the World League for Sexual Reform during the 1920s and early 1930s) who was a friend of Karl Giese and Magnus Hirschfeld, pioneers of Gay Liberation and curators of the Institut fur Sexualwissenschaft in Berlin (closed by the Nazis, its archives burned in May of 1933). A poignant token of the past to have found on a winter afternoon on a sidestreet of Copenhagen, a connection to other times and lives.

The subtle and elusive anguish that many Danes seem to nourish in their spirits has something to do with light, with the extremes of daylight from winter to summer, and the half-light of so many days. There would seem to be a more than casual connection between meteorology and metaphysics.

On autumn evenings you still can see itinerant knife and scissors grinders on side streets of the city, honing blades with their pedal-powered grinding wheels, sending sparks flying into the darkness. And on chill evenings organ grinders dressed in tophat and tails move their instruments slowly through the side streets, cranking out jolly tunes. People come to their windows to look and listen and send their children out with coins to put in the organ grinder's blue metal coffee pot.

In winter, the clochards of Copenhagen like to hang out in the city library on Krystalgade, where they doze in their overcoats with books open on their laps. The real saints of the city, though, are the old ladies who feed the birds, gulls, terns and pigeons, on the squares, and the ducks, swans and coots of the lakes, canals and parks. The birds recognize these thin, birdlike ladies who bring them bags of seed and suet and breadcrumbs day after day and at their approach there is great avian jubilation.

The winter days are cold, gray, dim, brief. When it grows sufficiently cold, children skate on the frozen lakes. On winter afternoons I like to sit on a bench beneath the dome of the grand old glass hothouse in the Botanical Gardens and breathe the warm, humid air among the tropical plants, the tall palm and banana trees. In winter I also relish sitting for hours in a café, the windows gray with condensation, warming my fingers on the cast iron radiator behind my chair, reading the Danish newspapers. Another agreeable indulgence I cultivate in winter is watching from my window the first electric commuter train of the morning (5:10 a.m.) As the pentagraph moves along the frost-coated overhead cable it makes a hissing, crackling, sputtering sound and produces livid flashes of light and a sun-bright spark of preternatural green.

In warmer weather, in common with other residents of the city, I like to sit with a coffee on a café terrrace and watch the endlessly mysterious and sometimes heartbreaking parade of humanity passing: beggars and beauties, lovers and loners, faces eager and defeated, gaily skipping children and muttering, shuffling old men, a phalanx of Japanese tourists, a man with parrots on his shoulders, a bald man wearing a dress, a stout woman in grimy finery pushing a baby carriage filled with her strange possessions. Everyone heading for somewhere.

In a secluded corner of an old park near the center of Copenhagen there is a curious sculpture to which I return again and again. The park was formerly the king's garden, a part of Rosenborg Castle. The statue, which represents a lion attacking a horse, is one of the oldest in the city, having been commissioned by King Christian IV in 1624. Peter Husum, the sculptor, had never seen a real lion and could thus only work after such contemporary pictorial depictions of the animal as were available to him, with the result that the face of his lion much more resembles that of a human being than the king of the beasts. But what engages my interest each time I visit the statue is that the expression in the eyes of the lion – who is engaged in biting and clawing the flesh of the horse's back – is one of profound melancholy, as if nothing occasioned him greater sorrow than his own violent appetites.

I am intrigued too by the carved faces and caryatids embellishing many of the older buildings of the city, not least the four stone figures above the entrance to the Danish Parliament building: four muscular but utterly doleful and disconsolate giants who are popularly said to represent earache, headache, stomachache and toothache. Elsewhere, throughout the city the most unsettling and grotesque carved visages of humans, demons and monsters gape and gloat, jeer and leer from the facades of buildings at passersby in the streets below. I often wonder what future archaeologists who excavate the ruins of Copenhagen will make of it.

Among the very first trees in Copenhagen to leaf each spring was the old horse chestnut known as the Holberg tree that stood in a walled court-yard on Fiolstræde, its branches rising above and reaching over the wall and overhanging the street. The tree was named for Ludvig Holberg (1684-1754), a Dano-Norwegian author who lived in the residence at number 8 Fiolstræde from 1740 until his death. Holberg is still admired here and abroad for his comedies (which owe something to those of Molière) but he was also the author of a curious and engaging book titled *The Journey of Niels Klim to the World Underground,* written in Latin and first published in 1741.

As the title suggests, the story concerns the adventures of a man named Niels Klim who falls through a hole in the earth and lands on the planet Nazar, a world within our world. Although primarily a social sat-ire, the story also possesses deeper resonances.

My favorite incident in the book is Niels Klim's encounter with the inhabitants of the Terrae Musicae whose bodies are half human and half bass viol, and whose speech consists of music which they play upon themselves. Under the solid gray, sullen skies of northern winter, you might almost conclude that you had fallen through a hole in the earth and landed in Denmark. Every year, for decades, I waited for the first spring leaves to appear on the Holberg tree. Then, one late summer day, I watched as two tree surgeons cut down the venerable old tree. Now, ev-ery time I pass the vacant place where it once stood, I mourn its absence. It was like losing a friend and seemed to me in some way to be the end of an era, an era that must have begun secretly long ago when a single horse chestnut seed germinated and took root in that place.

Riding on a commuter train in Copenhagen one day not long ago, reading a book, I came across a phrase from Aristotle pertaining to the state of foreigners and exiles: bios xenikon – the life of a stranger. I re-flected how the phrase fit my own life.

I am an American, from Arizona. I have lived here for many years, working as a gardener, a construction worker, a nightwatchman, a day laborer, a janitor, a private tutor, a freelance translator, a publisher's read-er, a research assistant and a part-time teacher.

I earn a modest and precarious livelihood and live with my wife in an impossibly small and unbearably noisy flat, the most recent and the worst in a series of cramped, cold, damp, draughty apartments with dripping faucets and running toilets and knocking pipes and creaking, clanking, whistling, gurgling radiators. These sounds can be borne; what is intoler-able is the noise of the other tenants, our immediate neighbors--their blar-ing, throbbing music, their raucous voices and the heavy tread of their Frankenstein feet as they lurch (back and forth, back and forth, back and forth, relentlessly, endlessly) across the snapping, cracking, straining wooden floorboards above our heads. From the flat above us you can hear every thump, bump, scrape and step, every slammed drawer and door, every urination, defecation and copulation, every conversation and argu-ment, every cough and sneeze, every giggle and guffaw, every word spo-ken, every object dropped. How often ruefully, wearily, we quote to each other Sartre's dictum: *l'enfer, c'est les autres.* [Hell is other people.]

Yet while it maddens the mind and burdens the spirit to have to exist in such demeaning straits, there are--strange to say—minor satisfactions of a kind to be derived from the challenges of chronic semi-penury. I take pleasure and a kind of pride in scrounging and foraging and finding things, activities akin, I suppose, to beachcombing. I buy my clothes at charity shops, searching with patience and persistence, selecting pants, shirts, socks, jackets, T-shirts, sweatshirts, handkerchiefs, often while served cups of coffee and cookies by the sweet-souled, white-haired la-dies who seem inevitably to run such places. At second-hand shops, flea markets and church bazaars, I find – in addition to clothes – towels, plates, cups, an iron and ironing board, a telephone, lamps, and other home furnishings. I also enjoy scavenging among throw-aways in the streets and bins, having found in this way numerous serviceable pots and pans, kitchen utensils, three radios, a wall clock with a wooden frame, desk chairs, wooden clothes hangers, picture frames, plentiful supplies of writing paper and envelopes, as well as many other useful objects. Pens and paper clips, I often find on streets and sidewalks, together with un-used bus tickets, coins, tools, even sleeping pills. (Oh, thank you, Lord!) Everything I find is something I don't have to buy.

The present, as we all know, quickly becomes the immediate past, then recedes in time and memory to an ever more distant past. Current events become history. Objects newly manufactured and regarded as use-ful and desirable, in time come to be seen as out-dated, are superceded in our affections, and are cast aside. In this manner, things once common become consigned to the periphery of our culture, unwanted, adrift on tides of chance, coming to grief and sinking into the seas of oblivion it may be or washing up at last on the shelves of junk shops and charity shops or on folding tables at flea markets. In such settings, for a time, the past persists: old clothes and shoes, old phonograph records, old maps and calendars, old teddy bears and dolls, old plates and cups and glasses, old postcards and photographs, old toys and children's games, old books and magazines. For what may be (for all I know) complex pyschological causes, I have long preferred the past to the present. And so – like a stranded mariner in search of sustenance on a desert isle – I forage among the jumble and clutter of bygone times ever in hope of a Proustian rush. To quote Montaigne: "The years can drag me along if they will, but they will have to drag me along facing backwards."

In the early 1970s, a number of American deserters began to drift across the sound from Sweden where they had been granted asylum ostensibly for reasons of conscience. Those of them I met and spoke with were on the run from the Swedish police for criminal offenses usually involving narcotics. Although they had secured sanctuary in Sweden by claiming opposition to the war in Vietnam, none of the deserters I met (not necessarily a representative sampling) were motivated by ideology or idealism of any kind. They had all as teenagers been in trouble with the law in the States and had been offered the choice of a prison term or enlisting in the army. Having chosen the latter, they had inevitably gotten into trouble again in the army and had ultimately deserted from posts in Germany to avoid court martial for serious offenses, usually theft.

Most often they were a sorry-ass lot, skinny, sullen, whiny and furtive, but one of them, John, who had a stiff leg and walked with a cane, was big-bellied and buoyant, a large, hearty, merry rogue. He had come to Copenhagen to "cool off" after a police raid on his Stockholm apartment during the course of which the police had pulled up the floorboards looking for his stash of saleable heroin (which he had with foresight concealed at his girl friend's apartment). A dealer and an occasional user of heroin, cocaine, speed and hashish, John's real preference was for alcohol and he would buy whiskey by the bottle from the bar and sit at a table drinking through whole afternoons and evenings. It was to whiskey he owed his stiff right leg, having while drunk and crossing a slushy Stockholm street been run down by a bus.

John's Swedish was very good and he told me that he had earned a good deal of money and something of a literary reputation as a writer of short stories for various Swedish magazines. His practice, he told me, was to visit the reading room of the Royal Library in Stockholm where he borrowed bound volumes of Esquire magazine from the 1940s and '50s. These he searched for stories by writers whose names he didn't recognize, translating their stories into Swedish and then marketing and selling them under his own name (I have since wondered whether this could be true).

John drifted back to Sweden when he reckoned that things had cooled off sufficiently for him to return and I saw him no more. But a few years later I heard from a Cockney friend of his that John had been murdered in Thailand, killed and robbed in the course of a dope deal he had gone there to transact. His Cockney friend still hoped to avenge him. "I'll get those bastards someday," he told me.

And there were other deserters in Copenhagen in the '70s, soldiers from other armies and other wars. I knew a shy, serious young Portugese student who had deserted from his country's army to avoid service in Angola. He had hidden himself in a duct above the bathroom of a passenger train and had ridden up through Spain, France, Belgium and Germany, arriving in Denmark after a journey of three days and three nights. The Danish government had granted him asylum. And there was Peter, a blue-eyed, boyish English deserter, a pacifist who had been conscripted into the British army and sent to Berlin.

There his pacifist statements and activities had aroused the anger of his commanding officer, who had arranged for him a "punishment posting" to Yemen, to a remote British outpost that came under nightly attack by insurgents. Surviving weeks of small arms fire and mortar attacks, Peter had contracted a severe form of dysentery and was sent for treatment to a British military hospital in Aden. Upon recovery, he deserted, making his way to Europe where he'd knocked around for some years before settling with his girlfriend in Copenhagen. Because of an Irish grandfather who'd come to England to work as a navvy and stayed to marry and father children, Peter was entitled to an Irish passport which enabled him to travel and to reside in Denmark as a citizen of the European Union. He remained an ardent pacifist (and vegetarian).

The oldest and angriest and saddest of the deserters I encountered in Copenhagen was Philip Tsirakides, a Greek-American who had been over the hill since 1944. Phil's dark, scarred Greek face wore a perpetual scowl, his lips pouted, his eyes had a fixed look of hostility. Only after you got to know him did you realize that beneath the challenging, menacing look in the brown eyes was a deeper expression of sorrow.

Phil had been drafted into the U.S. Army in early 1943, had served with the combat engineers in France and Germany, and had deserted in November of 1944. After six months of combat, he had been wounded and sent to a hospital, and after that he had had enough, he said. He went AWOL and spent the rest of the war in Paris and Brussels, surviving by stealing military supplies and selling them on the black market. Caught twice by the MPs and sent to disciplinary barracks, twice he had escaped. In late 1946 he was caught a third time, court-martialled and sentenced to twelve years confinement at hard labor. But before he could be returned to a federal prison in the United States to begin serving his sentence, again he escaped.

Avoiding his former haunts and contacts and cronies, Phil made his way to Berlin, where he soon joined a black market operation manufacturing and selling imitation penicillin. Ampoules filled with a mixture of dextrose and yellow face powder were sold as penicillin to prostitutes. After only six months, though, the German police, in co-operation with the British and American CID, arrested most of the gang, and Phil fled first to Paris, where he sold wool army blankets stolen from Graves Registration, and then to Tangier.

In Tangier he worked for an ex-GI American smuggler named Sydney Paley, running cigarettes and other contraband (including nylons) from Tangier to Spain, Malta, France and Italy, and participating in hi-jackings of competitors' ships. After Paley's arrest and deportation from Morocco, Phil served as an agent for the purchase and sale of looted and stolen Bearer Bonds. This lucrative enterprise enabled him to finance half a dozen other shady businesses in as many European countries.

Eventually, he acquired a Greek passport and a new name. He never returned to the United States, the country from which as a young man he sailed away to war so many years before. When I knew Philip Tsirakides he was a well-dressed, wary man in his early fifties with graying black hair combed straight back, hard eyes, tight lips and a scarred face. (The scars, he told me, were the result of a beating inflicted on him by MPs after his third capture in Liege). He was married to a Danish woman and was said to be running a small fleet of speed boats smuggling cigarettes and liquor into Sweden and Denmark. I believe he had illegal business interests elsewhere in Europe.

Phil's story came from him in episodes and fragments during the course of several night's drinking and smoking dope at Pilegaarden and Bobi-bar, then the favorite hang-outs of American and English expatriates in Copenhagen. I was a little afraid of him and was careful never to pry, but listened, nodding my head, maintaining eye contact, though his hard gaze sometimes caused a spasm at the back of my neck. One drunken night he told me his real motive for deserting from the army. It was not the war, he said, he could hack it, he could have gone back on the line. It was another thing, something that had bothered him and followed him since he entered the army and had gotten worse and worse until he couldn't stand it anymore. Other people had thought he was a negro, he said, and some of them hated him for it and rode him for trying to pass as a white man.

It had begun already when he was in basic training in Alabama. A southern drill sergeant had repeatedly singled him out for persecution and humiliation. On a weekend pass to a nearby town, two negro women had flirted with him. When he arrived in England, English children and English women had asked him if he was a "darkie." But worse than this was his platoon sergeant's undisguised contempt for him. Phil had hoped things would get better in combat, but in fact they had become worse.

Although he did his job as well as any other soldier in the unit, the sergeant never let up on him, riding him, calling him "boy" to his face and "nigger" behind his back, talking about him to other soldiers. He had tried to get a transfer to another unit but his c.o. had refused to consider it. So after recovering from his wounds, he had decided not to return to his unit. He would not endure such treatment. And he had never understood it, he said. He was not a negro, he was just a Greek, he looked no different than other Greeks he had grown up with.

I think, though, that however much and for however long he had wanted to tell someone about this inner injury, afterwards he must have felt ashamed or vulnerable and regretted having done so. When next we met I thought him more reserved with me and we spoke no more of his life. Some weeks later he left Copenhagen, together with his wife, and I never saw him again, nor ever learned what became of him on this earth.

But for my dear Danish wife, Birgit, I would not have remained in Denmark for more than a few years. Even now after having lived here for so many years this place seems cold and strange to me. I miss the heat and light of Arizona. I miss the vastness of America, the immense skies and horizons. (I often speculate whether Americans from the east can adapt to Europe more easily than westerners.) In any but the most strictly literal sense of the word, I am not an expatriate. Rather, I am a dislocated, a displaced person, an aging foreigner far from home.

Late nights I listen to the radio, slowly turning the tuning dial among the galaxies of stations in the European night, all the myriad of tongues and voices and musics. And yet I had lived here for many years before I discovered AFN (American Forces Network). It is a very weak signal and only becomes audible after 11 PM when the Russian station that overlaps its frequency signs off the air. Moreover, in order to receive AFN at all here in Denmark the radio must be turned to the southwest. The signal wavers and pulsates, hisses and whines, the reception is scratchy with static, at intervals it fades away altogether then slowly returns. But AFN is a kind of psychic lifeline to me. Night after night for many years I have listened to it, to oldtime radio programs rebroadcast on "Golden Days of Radio," to "American Country Countdown," to "Dr. Demento," to NPR news and "All Things Considered", to Jim Pewter's oldies show and Dick Clark's "Rock, Roll and Remembrance," and Laura Lee's "Jazz Beat," but the hours I most cherish on AFN are those broadcasting live satellite sports, and most especially baseball games. (Oh, Camden Yards, Wrigley Field, Riverfront Stadium, Fenway Park, Yankee Stadium, Tiger Stadium, Shea Stadium, and Edison Field, and oh players making the grab, swiping the bag, popping to short, or getting caught looking, oh the sinker, the slider, the heater, the change-up, oh spring games played in drizzle and games under the lights on balmly, muggy nights and Sunday afternoon games of late summer with the shadows of the light stanchions draped over the first base bag, and oh the long shadows of October advancing toward home plate.) And then in the Fall on AFN, football and serious talk of yardage and downs, tackles and penalties, wide receivers and interceptions, handoffs and incomplete passes, the I-formation, the shotgun, the snap, the blitz. And the announcers sending "a very special greeting" to all those around the world listening to the game on Armed Forces Network, "we hope we bring you a touch of home."

On nights of Labor Day and Thanksgiving and the Fourth of July, on rainy midnights or deep frozen winter nights or lying wakeful in the dark of the small hours, how I have been lifted to hear "The Parade of Sports" on AFN. What comfort it has given me, serving as a kind of aural "clean, well-lighted place", something to invoke against the void. And the wonder, the sheer strangeness and mystery of listening to distant disembodied voices, hearing what is said so far away by unseen persons you've never met nor ever shall meet, yet who have their own being, their own lives in the world, and the poignance of games played in the vastness of American afternoons and all the dreams and hopes and heartbreaks of America for which sports serve as a metaphor.

I have always relished the raffish and shabby, savored the louche and seedy sections of cities. Almost inevitably such quarters are zones of mystery and possibility, rich in encounters and artifacts. Like other dwindling resources, seediness should be carefully conserved, but everywhere the forces of militant banality advance and whole sections of Copenhagen have already fallen or are about to fall to their insipid assault. Gone now, irrevocably gone, is the authentic old Nyhavn quarter of rowdy sailor bars, ship's chandlers and tattoo parlors, the dark courtyards where drunken sailors vomited and the small hotels where they woke with hammering hangovers and last night's black eye. Today along Nyhavn, in haute cuisine restaurants, executives with cell phones eat pricey, dainty business lunches while tourists pass licking large ice-cream cones.

Gone too is disreputable old Teglgaardstræde with its gray-haired, grandmotherly prostitutes sitting rouged and powdered and be-lipsticked behind bay windows at street level or leaning out of second and third floor windows calling down to the passersby (and gone along with these venerable and stalwart harlots, two wonderful cluttered old bookshops and a cozy coffee-bar much frequented by Greenlanders down on their luck). A health food shop, a furniture store, a travel agency and chic clothes shops now occupy premises on Teglgaardstraede whose walls must once have absorbed the invisible energies of innumerable orgasms.

Only here and there in the city –like slowly withering oases – a handful of dingy, shabby shops selling disreputable goods yet survive. Fashionable boutiques, organic bakeries and overcute cafes are everywhere encroaching on Copenhagen's last repairs of seediness.

Between 1975 and 1993, Birgit and I (latterly with the heroic help of Lars Rasmussen of The Booktrader) put out 15 issues of an English-language literary journal called *Pearl*. Unprepossessing in appearance (printed by offset), it was, I like to think, distinguished in its contents. Contributors to *Pearl* included Kay Boyle, Robert Bly, Paul Bowles, Rita Dove, Charles Bukowski, William S. Burroughs, John Ciardi, Louis Simpson, Allen Ginsberg, David Ignatow, George Starbuck, Lawrence Ferlinghetti, Donald Hall, Denise Levertov, Charles Henri Ford, Joyce Carol Oates, Frederick Prokosch, Alan Sillitoe, George Barker, Christopher Logue, James Tate, and many others. W.H. Auden's literary executor sent us a previously unpublished sestina by Auden. Carolyn Cassady allowed us to print Neal Cassady's letters to her from prison. Norman Rubington sent us a new "Akbar del Piombo" collage narrative.

We had limited means and ultimately (with our ill-paid, uncertain jobs) we could no longer afford to print the magazine, (which ran at a deficit always). I hope that decades hence some enterprising, obsessive young collector of the expatriate literary past will discover yellowing copies of *Pearl* and will consider it a worthy artifact.

History happens and then for a time traces remain. On a little side-street near the center of the city there is a tavern where in a wall behind the bar you can still see a bullet hole made in April of 1944 when two members of a Danish resistance group shot dead a man they knew to be an informer. Lonely, bored German *wehrmacht* sentries standing guard at buildings near the switching yards of the central railway station scratched dates, initials, names and messages into the yellow brick walls of a warehouse. (Very likely at night and out of sight of their NCOs and officers.) On one brick a melancholy soldier scratched: "Weinachten 1943 auf posten." (Christmas Eve 1943 on duty). He must have thought longingly of his family in Germany that cold evening in Copenhagen and of the dear Christmases of his childhood. On a brick nearby, another hapless soldier's hand has engraved a subversive riposte to Joseph Goebbels infamous "Sportpalast Speech" of February 1943, where Goebbels posed to his carefully selected audience the rhetorical question: "Do you want

total war?" In response, this anonymous German soldier has left us a record of his sense of disenchantment and disillusion: "Wolt ihr den totalen
krieg? Nein." (Do you want total war? No.) Strange traces yet remaining
of lives lived long ago – eyes that saw a world once, hands, minds.

I stand at a school bus stop in Copenhagen and note names and dates
scratched into the bricks of a wall: Karin 1947, Kaj 1950, Humle 1951,
Knold 1959, Maj 1961, Ann 1963. Where are they now, I wonder, the
boys and girls who once affirmed in this manner their existence in time?
And I wonder if any of those who scratched their name and the date into
the brick ever returns to see it again or touch it with their fingers and remember the hour and the day they engraved it there?

In the streets of the city, the faces and lives and fates. The old cobblestones, the weathered, discolored brick. The swifts diving and whistling
above the chimneys in the long summer dusk. Gray autumn sky and the cry
of a seagull. The shallow arc of the winter sun, the cold slant of winter
sunlight in the streets. The faces and lives and fates in the streets of the city.

Calling on Paul Bowles
Tangier, Morocco, August 1979

"There it is," someone says, and in the darkness, in the distance, you can see Tangier sprawled across several hills, a white city illuminated by electric lights and veiled by a thin fog.

After docking, disembarking and a wearisome wait to clear Moroccan customs, we take a taxi to our hotel, hurtling through the midnight streets of Tangier past Ramadan revelers and bright cafés. At the hotel, a desk clerk denies all knowledge or record of our reservation until Birgit produces from her purse a letter of confirmation. We are shown to a room and soon fall into an exhausted sleep. (The previous night at a hotel in Malaga we had been kept awake until 4.30 a.m. by a raucous party taking place in the room next door to ours, and were then awoken at 7 a.m. by a phone call from a furious desk clerk berating us for having caused the commotion and ordering us out of the hotel immediately. He wouldn't stop yelling long enough for me to assert our innocence.)

I wake in the dark, hauled up from deep strata of sleep. In the street below a dog is barking. The bark is deep, resonant and insistent, the bark of a big dog and very near. On and on he barks. Long minutes pass. I despair of sleep. Then, from the street there is the sharp report of a firearm being discharged. A single loud shot, then silence. "My God," I think, "this really is a tough town." Hours later I wake to the muezzin's call to prayer.

We spend the day wandering in the medina, or old city. In the evening we walk to the Inmeuble Itesa, an anonymous concrete building on the outskirts of Tangier where Paul Bowles lives. We ascend to the fourth floor, ring the bell and are admitted by Bowles who greets us by name. We are expected and welcome, he says.

A few years before our visit we had written to Paul Bowles, soliciting a contribution to our literary journal, *Pearl*. He kindly obliged by sending us a poem. An exchange of letters ensued in the course of which he extended to us an invitation to call upon him in Tangier. When (after about 18 months) we accepted, he provided us with his street address which was not the same as his postal address.

We enter and shake hands and are offered tea. Black tea with slices of lemon, served in cups of thick transparent glass. Bowles' modest but modern apartment consists of three or four rooms. There is a hallway stacked with old suitcases, a small kitchen, and a dim bedroom with an adjoining bathroom. The living room is furnished with low wooden tables, colored cushions for sitting and a low couch. There is a fireplace, a shelf of books and a large studded wooden chest. The floors are covered with red, black and tan Moroccan rugs. Leaning against the walls are framed paintings by Ahmed Yacoubi and Mohammed Mrabet. On the mantel and the tables are placed objects of hammered brass and an antique long-stemmed, small-bowled, silver oriental water pipe. Outside, but visible from the living room, there is a balcony crowded with tall plants.

Bowles is a slender man with blue eyes and thick white hair. He is dressed with casual elegance in well-fitting clothes, a white Moroccan-style shirt and tan slacks. On the little finger of his right hand, he wears two gold rings. He chain smokes kif cigarettes from a black cigarette holder.

We have brought with us from Denmark gifts for Bowles: two black leather notebooks, a stone wear bottle of Danish mead and a pound of black tea steeped in the juice of blackcurrants. He receives these graciously, inspects them carefully and pronounces himself eager to try the tea whose fragrance he inhales with obvious interest and approval. He asks us our impressions of Tangier so far. We are both ardent in our praise of the city, especially the medina. We've never seen anything comparable. Bowles smiles and seems pleased by our naive enthusiasm. "You weren't annoyed by the touts?" he asks with concern. We assure him that we were courteously firm with them and did not find them bothersome. Again, he seems pleased, even relieved, as if he considers himself responsible for our having a good time in Tangier or as if he is anxious that his city (as it were) might arouse aversion in some visitors.

Bowles offers us kif cigarettes which we accept and he then discourses on kif, saying that it should be bought fresh and that ideally one should prepare ones own kif, chopping the dried cannabis leaves into a fine powder and mixing the powder with an appropriate amount of tobacco in order to achieve a congenial blend. Some professional cutters of kif are highly skilled, others less so.

Accordingly, their product varies in quality. The hashish available in Tangier is of very poor quality, he says, consisting of the leftover leaves of the cannabis plant after the small potent kif leaves have been carefully removed. Bowles forms kif cigarettes for his own use by emptying the tobacco from a Marlboro and then filling the paper cylinder with the fresh mountain-grown kif he has recently purchased in the marketplace from wonted and reliable vendors. He stores the kif intended for his immediate use in a small round red container which he keeps close at hand.

Madame Claude Nathalie Thomas arrives and speaks with Bowles concerning her translation of certain of his short stories. Mohamed Choukri (whose book *A Life Full of Holes* was dictated to and translated by Paul Bowles) comes to call. A dark-haired, sad-eyed man, he engages Bowles in a conversation in Spanish. Then, soon after Choukri's arrival, Mohammed Mrabet makes his entrance, immediately compelling attention by his energy, his intensity and an aura of danger that he projects. Directly, he seizes the conversation (speaking Spanish, ignoring Choukri) and thereafter keeps it in his possession.

Mrabet is a handsome, agile, mobile, muscular man about 40 years of age. He is dressed in faded blue jeans and a bright orange short-sleeved shirt with vivid paisley trimmings. With his heavy finger rings and his large silver wrist watch, there is about him something of the air of a brigand or Barbary pirate, flashy and fierce. Birgit and I know and admire his writing and have brought some gifts for him, but I'm embarrassed to give them to him in the presence of Mohamed Choukri, so I wait for an opportunity to take him aside.

At length, as Mrabet seems to be leaving, I succeed in speaking to him alone and off to one side. I know that he does not speak English and since I don't speak Spanish I address him in French. I tell him that we esteem his books and I present him with the gifts we've brought: an ornate Spanish pocket knife, a jar of dark Danish heather honey, and a pound of the same black tea flavored with blackcurrant that we've brought for Bowles. Mrabet is touched and pleased with the gifts. He thanks us and promises that he will soon return. He must first make a quick visit to his mother.

Mohamed Choukri leaves and Madame Thomas also leaves. Bowles plays tapes of Moroccan music and percussive, oriental-sounding music by an American composer named Lou Harrison. We smoke kif and drink tea and Bowles eats a late dinner of soup, rice and chicken. He tells us that he eats only two meals a day, breakfast and dinner. He gets dizzy sometimes, he says, adding with a smile that it may be that the kif he smokes all day contributes to this condition. I ask him if he has kept up with developments in jazz since his days as a music critic in New York. No, he replies, his knowledge of jazz effectively ends in the mid 1940s before the advent of bebop. He still respects Duke Ellington as a composer and a conductor. He found Ellington's musical ideas very inventive, his band expressive and exciting. Other individual musicians whose work he admired during the 1940s included Fats Waller, the pianist Albert Ammons, the guitarist Charlie Christian, the alto saxophonist Johnny Hodges, as well as the pianists James P. Johnson and Teddy Wilson. But since moving to Morocco he has, of course, been unable to attend live performances while access to current recordings is difficult and expensive.

Mrabet returns with a delicious Ramadan desert made by his mother which we enjoy with fresh tea and more kif. When Mrabet has smoked a sufficient amount of kif he begins to recount personal anecdotes, one after another. For our sake, these are related by him in French. The majority of his narratives on this occasion consist of angry stories involving betrayal and revenge. As he speaks, he is animated, passionate, the veins standing out on his neck. He believes he has been poisoned by his former wife. He believes that she tricked him into eating finely ground glass mixed into his food. Only recently his stomach has been operated on and while he was in the hospital his wife destroyed all his belongings, killing his pets and even his plants. But again and again he insists "Je suis content." (I'm happy.) He claims that he has accepted and transcended his sufferings. He believes that one should return good for evil, the more evil done against one, the more good must be done in return, a ratio of ten to one. Mrabet also recounts how one of his brothers killed his wife, spent 13 years in prison, then upon release engaged in further crimes and knifings until at last he was killed. Life is full of suffering, he says. He has himself suffered much, but then he adds *"Je suis content."*

As we make to leave, thanking our host, we ask him to sign our copy of *Let It Come Down,* an English first edition of the book. Bowles studies the dust wrapper with interest and seems somehow impressed that we have with us this particular copy. Why don't we return for it tomorrow? he suggests. We are welcome to call on him every evening during our stay in Tangier, he says.

We are surprised and deeply pleased, having thought that his invitation to visit him was for a single call, a single evening. (When the next evening Bowles returns the book to us, signed and inscribed, he asks us humbly if we enjoyed the novel. Oh yes, yes, very much, we tell him and he beams with pleasure.) Mrabet drives us to our hotel. En route he tells us of his deep affection for Bowles and that if Bowles should die it will mean the end of Mrabet as a writer, since it is Bowles who translates his stories into English. And he has an ominous feeling concerning the present state of Bowles' health; he fears Bowles may be sick. In any event, Mrabet estimates that they may have only two productive years of work together remaining.

Fascinated by the medina, we return there again and again during our days in Tangier. The white flat-roofed buildings, the steep narrow streets in sharp light and shadow, the shops, stalls, small cafés, the souks and bazaars, the men in hooded brown djellabas, the veiled Arab women in black robes, blue robes and white robes, the Berber women with their wide-brimmed, high-crowned straw hats, their shawls, their red and white striped skirts, the pavements of cobble stone and brick, the windows with their pointed arches, the white-washed walls, the wooden doors, the blue shutters, the wrought iron balconies and grilles, the stairways and dark alleys, the awnings and tiled doorways, the arched passageways and impasses, the shoe-shine boys and beggars, the vendors of lottery tickets, the peddlers, the water seller in his tasseled straw hat with his brass cups and goat skin water bag, the shuffling slippers and sandals in the winding streets. The children's' shoes arranged outside a small Koranic school, the cross-legged tailors, the carpenters hammering and sawing in their narrow shops, the candies, cashews and almonds piled in heaps, the ceramics, brass and copper, the leather goods, the melons, the metal and plastic buckets filled with Barbary figs, the spices, cloth, fresh meat, onions, goat cheese, the fruits and vegetables and eggs. The odor of rat poison in the Kasbah. The taste of sweet mint tea at the Café Centrale. And lying at intervals here and there, face up in the dusty streets -- like a fortune teller's scattered spread – castaway Baraja playing cards with their strange tarot-like suits and symbols.

Bowles picks us up at our hotel in his gold 1965 Ford Mustang, driven by his chauffeur, Abdelouahid Boulaich, a trim, balding man. Bowles and Abdelouahid converse in Spanish. We are driven west along a winding road, out of the city, up into the mountains, past luxurious villas and into a forest of eucalyptus, pine, cypress and jacaranda. We follow a dirt road through the forest, park the car and walk to a large lichen-splattered rock perched above the sea. The breeze is fresh and fragrant. The air is vibrant with the whine of cicadas. "This is my favorite spot," Bowles says. Below us in the distance we can see goats grazing the slopes and children fishing in the sea. We walk paths thick with pine needles and approach the Villa Perdicaris whose owner Ion Perdicaris, together with his son-in-law, was kidnapped and held for ransom by the Berber bandit Mulai Ahmeder Raisuli in 1904.

This incident proved to have repercussions far beyond Morocco as Perdicaris was at first believed to be an American citizen. President Theodore Roosevelt dispatched a fleet of warships to the coast of Morocco, pressuring the Sultan and demanding "Perdicaris alive or Raisuli dead." Raisuli's demands were met by the Sultan, Perdicaris and his son-in-law freed, while Raisuli went on to become Pasha of Tangier and governor of Jibala province. Bowles smiles as he tells us that a recent Hollywood film ("The Wind and the Lion" starring Sean Connery and Candace Bergen) treating the Perdicaris incident has been made in which the victim of the bandit's kidnapping is a woman while the bandit Raisuli is portrayed as a noble rebel fighting tyrannous oppression. Bowles has not seen the film, he says, but he has read of it.

The Villa Perdicaris itself is a large Gothic sort of house with crenellated towers. It is abandoned and in a condition of disrepair. We drive to Cape Spartel where the waters of the Mediterranean meet those of the Atlantic Ocean. Palm, broom, cork-oak and eucalyptus abound here. A solitary lighthouse is situated on a promontory overlooking the vast Atlantic. During our journey together, I note that Bowles (once a noted composer) frequently whistles elusive musical passages or taps out rhythms on the dashboard or with his arm out the window on the roof of the car. Are these habits, I wonder, outward expressions of rhythms and harmonies he might be hearing in the privacy of his mind, tokens of a sort of interior musical monologue? I recall reading a comment by Ned Rorem who – regretting the fact that Bowles had abandoned his work as a composer – pronounced a hope that "Someday Bowles may release the underestimated musician who doubtless still sings within him."

That evening in Bowles' kitchen, Mrabet prepares for us a Moroccan *tagine*, a delicious stew of chicken, onions, olives and mushrooms, served with a wonderful brown bread baked by Mrabet's mother. In respect for Ramadan, we wait until the sunset cannon has been fired, then we eat seated on the floor around the living room and even Bowles eats heartily. Bowles plays tapes of Moroccan music that he has recorded just outside his window. After dinner, kif is smoked and Mrabet tells numerous stories. These include the tale of a queen and a golden chain, the story of a baker who found a diamond, and the story of a poem that came to Mrabet while he was in jail: "Breast on breast/With your hair disheveled/ Bought a ring/worth two ships/My gazelle/The ships have sailed."

At Bowles' suggestion, Mrabet also relates to us the story of how he discovered a magic bundle hidden in the soil of a potted plant in Jane Bowles' apartment. (Birgit and I have already read of this incident but are fascinated to hear it related by the principals.) One night Mrabet had dreamed of the presence of something evil in one of the potted plants in Jane Bowles' house in the medina. The following day he deliberately visited the house and attempted to examine the plant, but he was attacked by Cherifa, Jane Bowles' Berber housekeeper, who drove him away with blows and curses.

This behavior on the part of Cherifa confirmed Mrabet's suspicion that some form of black magic was being perpetrated on Jane by Cherifa. With the help of Paul Bowles, Mrabet succeeded in removing the plant, a stunted philodendron, to Bowles' apartment. There, Mrabet examined the plant, finding a cloth packet buried among its roots, a packet composed of black magical ingredients intended by Cherifa to exercise a spell over Jane Bowles. This was not the first instance of Cherifa having planted about the house black magic packets. Mrabet considered her a witch and believed her to be responsible for Jane Bowles' illness, both through magic and poisoning. Birgit and I are shown the very same philodendron plant on Bowles' balcony, now large and thriving.

Bowles adds that this was neither the first time, nor the last, that Mrabet had dreamed true regarding Jane. On one occasion, he says, Mrabet had dreamed that Jane have given him a gold coin on a chain, and not long afterward such a gift had, indeed, been given to Mrabet by Jane. On another occasion, Mrabet had related to him a dream in which Mrabet had seen Jane Bowles holding a flower. There was something ominous and disagreeable about the flower, Mrabet had said. Mrabet was convinced that the dream portended some impending disaster that would befall Jane. Soon thereafter Bowles had received an urgent telegram from the clinic in Malaga where Jane was being treated. He was informed that her condition had worsened and had become critical. He traveled there with all haste, only barely reaching her side before she died. In this case, too, Mrabet's unconscious intuition had proved to be accurate.

Again, by pre-arrangement, Bowles calls for us at our hotel and we are driven in his Ford Mustang by Abdelouahid Boulaich, traveling east out of Tangier. The goal of our excursion is to be shown Abdelouahid's house, a house which he has been constructing by himself and which is now sufficiently compete for both him and his wife to occupy. The terrain is arid and hilly, rock-strewn and brown. Cattle and goats graze on shrubs. There are prickly pear cacti and agave plants. Many of the latter have bloomed and are now dead as signaled by their tall, dry stalks. Overhead, in the blue air, a buzzard hovers, slowly circling. We pass Berber countrywomen in their broad straw hats, leading laden donkeys. Cattle are driven along the road by boys with sticks. In a field, a flock of camels stands and reclines. The afternoon is bright and silent. The only sounds are the whine of cicadas, the baaing of goats, the crowing of cocks. Along a tree-lined road, farmers, their dogs and donkeys are resting in the shade.

Bowles points out to us the tomb of Sidi Ali, purple, gray massive Jebel Musa (the southern pillar of Hercules) and the ruined Portugese fort at Ksar es Seghir. We follow narrow dirt roads to the hillside house of Abdelouahid. The exterior of the house is white, the flat roof is crenellated to resemble a fortress. There are wrought iron grilles on the windows. The interior is cool but we stand and sit outside on a walled porch paved with flagstones. Abdelouahid serves us mint tea and fresh figs, but after a few wary sips Bowles remarks that the tea tastes strange. He believes that standing water must have been used to make the tea. He consults with Abdelouahid in Spanish and the tea is removed. After an interval, Abdelouahid returns with a new pot of mint tea made with fresh water and Bowles pronounces it "perfecto."

From our vantage on the hillside we can see the brown coast of Spain across the Strait of Gibraltar. I mention the memorial in Algeciras commemorating the landing there of General Franco and his army in 1936. Bowles recounts how Franco brought with him to Spain many thousand Moroccan troops, both conscripts and volunteers. Those Moroccans who joined usually did so to escape desperate poverty. "Los Moros" (the Moors) as the Spanish called the Moroccan troops inspired terror among the Spaniards. Their method of fighting, he says, was merciless, involving the indiscriminate killing of civilians. This practice was deliberately exploited by Franco as a means to subdue the Spanish population. In consequence, there is still a lingering ill-will toward Moroccans on the part of many Spaniards.

I tell Bowles that Birgit and I have over the years assembled our collection of his works (many of them out-of-print) by scouring used book shops around Europe, acquiring some of his books in unlikely circumstances. He recalls with fondness the stalls of the *bouquinistes* along the Seine where he found many curious and unusual books as well as back issues of the handsomely produced surrealist magazine, *Minotaure,* and other avant-garde literary journals. Indeed, it was in a similar manner, he says, that he garnered his early collection of jazz and blues records, finding them in secondhand furniture stores.

We talk of the remarkable art work done by untutored Moroccan painters such as Ahmed Yacoubi and Mohamed Hamri, both of whom early in their careers had been encouraged by Bowles. I mention that one of Hamri's paintings is featured on the dust jacket of the English edition of Brion Gysin's novel, *The Process.* "Ah yes, *The Process,"* Bowles says with a faint smile, suggesting that he esteems that book very little. Hamri, he relates, had earned his living as a smuggler and a house painter before ever applying paint to canvas. Unfortunately though not surprisingly, he says, Hamri had stolen a number of personal possessions from Gysin and from Bowles, too, though both men had befriended and encouraged him in his career as an artist, even providing him with art supplies. Bowles observes that Moroccans view foreigners as quarry, as a resource to be turned to economic account or utilized for some other advantage. This fundamental attitude on their part, he says, has been inherited by them from the time of the Barbary pirates.

In making such a pronouncement upon the behavior of Moroccans, Bowles evinces neither animus nor contempt, but rather an attitude of resignation to the inevitable. His perspective on humanity – its customs and behaviors – resembles that of a kind of ethnographer or anthropologist. He observes, remains objective, withholds moral judgment. He is intrigued by human passion and vanity, bemused without being condescending. His characteristic physical posture, that of a relaxed yet attentive poise, also suggests this view of things. A common denominator underlying many of his remarks (concerning the decline of Tangier, the decline of Europe and the United States, the decline of travel, the decline of the quality of food, for example) is that we should be under no illusion concerning the character of the era we live in and the world we inhabit;

we ought to have a clear, unblinking look at existence and phenomena but we must also accept that the state of things is irremediable.

We return to Tangier along the winding coast road. Distant misty mountains to the south. Blue sea breaking white on beaches to the north. Above us, an immensity of empty sky. Even on this short trip, scanning the landscape from the front seat of his chauffeur-driven car, Bowles seems in his element, intent, alert, the consummate traveler.

We're taking a late-afternoon nap in our hotel room when the phone rings. It's the desk clerk. "Mrabet est ici," he says. (Mrabet is here.) I descend the stairs to the lobby, shake hands with Mrabet and ask him to come up to our room. He invites us to his mother's house for dinner, to eat the fish that he has caught this afternoon at Ksar es Seghir.

Arriving at the house, we are introduced to Mrabet's mother who in courteous Moroccan fashion after shaking our hands touches her open hand to her heart. We are served sweet mint tea and then share kif cigarettes with Mrabet (hand rolled by him using two Job papers) while listening to audio cassettes of *chleuh* music – pipes, string instruments, flutes, drums, singing. Mrabet tells us that kif smokers prefer *chleuh* music, *jilala* music or *gnaua* music. There was a time, he says, when particular forms of music caused him to enter a trance state, even against his will. Hearing such music he could not resist being drawn into a condition of unconsciousness while his body remained awake and active. While in this state, which might last for hours, he often injured himself. He has since trained himself to resist the music, he says, but he is still susceptible to the odor of *bakhour,* an incense. In spite of his best efforts to withstand its influence, the smell of *bakhour* will induce in him a trance state.

The three of us sit on the floor around a low round table and eat from a large common dish, using Mrabet's mother's excellent bread to maneuver our food. The first course is sheep liver in a spiced sauce. This is followed by Mrabet's fish, a large sea bass, then flan for desert. After this delicious dinner, further kif cigarettes elicit from Mrabet a stream of stories. "I always tell stories at this time of night," he says. He adds that when he is not smoking kif he becomes quiet and fat-faced. Once, he tells us, he abstained for the length of a year from smoking kif. He became nearly unrecognizable to his friends and even to his family. At last he accepted a pipe of kif from a friend and his friend looked with amazement at the sudden transformation of Mrabet's face, exclaiming: "Ah, that's the real Mrabet!"

One of Mrabet's stories this evening concerns Birgit. She ate a loaf of bread as big as the sky then to quench her thirst drank seven rivers. Mrabet went to the market and bought a pomegranate that weighed five kilos but in attempting to bear it to his house he fell under the weight of it. The pomegranate broke in two. One of the halves had a door which he opened and entered, finding there a palace. Exploring the palace, he discovered a room full of honey. There he killed a large mosquito and filled its headless body with honey. He then flung the honey-filled mosquito across his shoulder, carrying it like a sack. However, attempting to cross a river, he accidentally dropped his burden, thereby sweetening the water. Exiting from the door he had entered in the broken pomegranate, he now noticed a door in the other half. He opened the door, entered, "and there you were, Birgit!" Ending his tale in this fashion, Mrabet laughs his customary curious and disconcerting laugh.

Mrabet's strange laugh begins as a flash of teeth and eyes, followed by a rattle in the throat, a wheezing of the lungs. Then his eyes close and his face assumes an agonized grimace, the corners of his open mouth turned down like a mask of tragedy as he sobs with mirth. Even his saddest stories conclude with this laugh as if they are a sort of joke on the listener or as if life is a kind of joke on the living.

Mrabet sets great store by dreams. He is impressed when Birgit tells him that she dreamed that he visited us. "Tu as un bon coeur," he tells her.

(You have a good heart.) He makes her a gift of a silver chain with a silver coin on which there is a likeness of King Mohammed V. He loved Mohammed V, he tells us, truly loved him, and he suspects his son, the current king, Hassan II, of having had a hand in his sudden death. Accordingly, he has neither love nor respect for Hassan and feels himself estranged from the king and his entire administration. Mrabet has himself had an alarming dream, only last night. He dreamed that while combing his hair things began falling from his scalp, including three lice. He is convinced that this dream bodes ill for him and the prospect of impending misfortune troubles his thoughts.

Mrabet drives us to his café. The walls of the café are decorated with his paintings and drawings. Moroccan men sit at tables, drinking coffee, coca cola and glasses of mint tea, smoking, playing cards and parcheesi. On the television screen there is a religious discussion among bearded imams.

A strangely subdued Mrabet calls for us at our hotel. The intrigues and betrayals of his wife still weigh heavily upon him, he explains. Moreover, last night there was an incident in his café. An aggressive drunk came in and began at once to create a disturbance. Ultimately, the man knocked down Mrabet's crippled waiter who then phoned Mrabet. Mrabet arrived and duly punched out the drunk. But the police intervened and took both of them to the police station where Mrabet had remained for long hours. Today, his right hand is swollen and sore. I note that he has moved his rings to the fingers of his left hand.

Mrabet wants us to see the town of Asilah. We drive south and west out of Tangier, bouncing along dirt roads in Mrabet's dusty, battered, brown Ford Fairlane, a Bob Marley cassette playing. He tells us that he has nearly completed a new book to be titled *Night Honey.* It is the story of his terrible marriage and the sufferings that followed. "If you have a heart, you'll weep when you read it," he says.

Mrabet prides himself on his self-sufficiency, his independence. He can provide for all his wants and needs, he says. He traps birds to sell, he fishes, he hunts, he slaughters his own livestock, butchers his own meat, cooks his own meals. He is also fiercely proud that his family is from the Rif. He likes to be called "El Rifi" and often uses this name for autobiographical alter-ego figures in his novels and tales. The people from the Rif are the best people, he says, the cleanest and strongest, the most upright and pious, and the kif plants grown in the mountains there make the best kif.

Fierce light and the shrill, relentless whine of cicadas. Corn fields, rows of prickly pear, the tower of a distant mosque. The road suddenly crowded with cattle. And along the roadside, sheep, camels, goats, donkeys. Through a village, Had e Rabiah, and then to our right the blue sea under a wide blue sky. Railroad tracks, a sulfurous stench and then we are in Asilah. We walk the medina, the ramparts, view a crumbling Portugese fort, the tomb of Sidi Mansour. In the market, melons, peppers, tomatoes, squash, cactus figs, fish, crabs, hens. A ragged, turbaned, white-bearded old man sits on the ground with strange desert refuse displayed before him on a blanket. An old revolver dissolving in rust, broken dirt-clogged clay pipe bowls, tarnished brass cartridge cases. Fascinated by the man and his desert debris, I purchase some of his wares, counting dirham coins into his palm.

On the return trip to Tangier, Mrabet tells us that he makes daily calls on Paul Bowles. Indeed, he sometimes visits him as many as six times in a day. If you are friends then it should be that way, he says. You should see your friend every day even if only for a few minutes. He tells us that sometimes he may be engaged in repairing something or driving his car when suddenly he feels he should go to see Bowles. At such moments he fears that something may have happened to him. Sometimes, Mrabet says, he cleans Bowles' apartment when the maid fails to appear. Some days she has to visit her son in jail and, of course, Bowles has no telephone.

In our hotel room we smoke kif cigarettes with Mrabet and view his photo album. There are photographs of Mrabet on the beach, young and muscular. There are photographs of relatives and childhood friends, his benefactors Russ and Anne-Marie Reeves, and his friends Paul and Jane Bowles. He was very fond of Jane Bowles, he tells us. He felt very close to her and her illness and death saddened him deeply. Mrabet repeatedly remarks that he feels he is now only a shadow of his former self, the younger Mrabet depicted in the photographs. Bad living (he used to drink alcohol) and misfortunes have weakened him. "I swear to you, I had fantastic strength;" he says ruefully, "if I had met Hercules I could have made *salade niçoise* of him."

Then, Mrabet is off to the market to do his shopping: "a donkey's ear, cloud butter, powdered water and a frog's gallbladder." He laughs in gasps while his face shapes a mask of tragedy.

Evenings in Bowles' apartment unfold according to an implicit, organic pattern. There is black tea and kif, conversation, oral tales spontaneously composed by Mrabet. Late in the evening, cold melon is served. On these occasions, Mrabet plays the mischievous jester; he is the performer, the prodigy and protégé. He thrives on attention. Bowles is the observer, reserved, reticent, restrained. Bowles seems, as Birgit remarks to me, rather like a fondly indulgent parent where Mrabet is concerned. (Bowles is without offspring, Mrabet was thrown out of his home by his father.) Or is their friendship something on the order of that between Ishmael and Queequeg?

Mrabet's tales often begin firmly anchored in a realistic, recognizable world with details of place and time, then take a surreal turn and become strange, poetic fables. For example, he begins: "I used to work at the docks unloading the ships and every morning I drank my coffee and ate my pastry at the same café and every morning the same woman passed by." Mrabet then introduces into the story the image of a hair in a box worth 10,000 francs, a boat built of smoke, a talking tree.

We view a portfolio of Mrabet's paintings and drawings which is owned by or stored with Bowles. The motifs are rendered in contrastive colors and intricate detail, creating a hallucinatory effect. There are faces, snakes, eyes, plants, birds, animals and spirit entities. The visionary, mythic quality of the work brings to my mind the art of the Huichol and the Tarahumara in Mexico.

When I mention the Tarahumara, Bowles says that he once translated some Tarahumara myths for a surrealist magazine. He rummages in his bedroom and returns with a copy of *View* for May 1945, a special "Tropical Americana" number which he edited. There are black and white photographs, collages and translations, including sections of the *Popul Vuh* and the *Chilam Balam,* all done by Bowles. A myth titled "John Very Bad" has been rendered by him into English from the Tarahumara. There are also bizarre and gruesome news stories selected by Bowles from the Mexican press.

Bowles speaks of the extreme poverty and squalor he encountered in parts of Mexico when he visited that country in the 1930s. Mexico was a land of gloom and chaos, he says, but also poetry, mystery and great natural beauty. Places such as Acapulco and Tehuantepec were very pleasant in those days and living there was very cheap. Yet he was often very ill in Mexico, afflicted with diverse ailments.

I ask Bowles if he ever thinks of returning to the countries he visited as a young man or of traveling to other regions of the globe. He dare not leave Morocco, he says. He is afraid that if he leaves the Moroccan authorities will revoke his residence permit or will not renew it. The reason for this state of affairs, Bowles explains, is that his books and his translations have offended elements of the ruling elite of Morocco. They have concluded that some of his fiction and the works he has translated by Larbi Layachi, Choukri and Mrabet reflect ill on Morocco. The authorities have succeeded in banning the sale of certain of these writers in Morocco. Copies of their books have been confiscated by the police and destroyed. It is a very sensitive issue. The western-educated political elite refuses to acknowledge that such conditions and such people as portrayed in these writings still exist. The ruling elite wants to promote abroad the image of Morocco as a modern country.

If he were to be expelled from Morocco or denied re-entry, he would not know where to go. Everywhere else seems unappealing. Even though Tangier has certainly changed for the worse over the years, he says, it still remains far less objectionable than any other place he can imagine.

In this regard, I mention that we found Madame Porte's café (a Tangier landmark) closed this afternoon but there was no indication whether the closure was merely temporary or permanent. Ominously, though, the café looked abandoned. An elegant place, Bowles says, with excellent cakes and cookies. Madame Porte was rumored to have been a collaborationist, he adds. "I put her into *Let It Come Down,* she says *Guten abend."*

I mention to Bowles that, like him, I am an admirer of Kurt Schwitters and his *Merz* collages. Bowles brightens at the mention of Schwitters. "I stayed with him and his family in their apartment in Hannover," he recalls. "I even helped him to gather materials for his collages." He esteemed Schwitters as an independent spirit and a man of creative integrity. Inspired by one of Schwitters' sound poems, Bowles says, he wrote a passage in a musical composition titled *Sonata for Oboe and Clarinet.*

Another artist whose work Bowles admires, he tells us, is the French painter, Jean Dubuffet (not to be confused with Bernard Buffet). He finds in Dubuffet's paintings a subversive spirit akin to that of Schwitters. Both Schwitters and Dubuffet can be credited with originality and authenticity in their response to the myriad horrors of the modern world.

Certain affinities, he says, can also be seen between works by Dubuffet and those of Mrabet, and, indeed, the art of the Tarahumara and others. Such works seem to have their origin in a common state of consciousness or mode of perception, in secret and mysterious resources of the mind.

We observe that we find it curious that none of Bowles' stories or novels have ever been filmed. This is strange since so many works by his literary contemporaries have appeared in film adaptations. Have screen rights for any of his fiction been purchased? Bowles replies that of his four novels he has sold the screen rights to all but *The Spider's House.* The screen plays for *The Sheltering Sky, Let It Come Down* and *Up Above the World*, had, however, all been very badly written and no-one was interested in filming them. Bowles says that he is entirely content with this state of things because at the time that he sold the screen rights, "my wife was very ill," and the money he received was welcome. Perhaps, too, it is just as well that none of the novels have ever been filmed, he adds, since you can't know what the director will do with the characters and the story. After selling the screen rights the author has no rights whatever concerning the cinematic adaptation of his work. He had once accompanied Tennessee Williams to a screening of *Boom,* (a film based on a play by Williams) and Williams had been appalled and depressed by what the director had made of his play.

Bowles smiles with grim amusement in telling us that in the contemporary world movies and show business would seem largely to have supplanted literature. His own literary agents in New York, he says, now describe themselves on their letterhead as "Agents to the Stars." This minor but telling alteration from a literary agency to an entertainment agency serves to confirm his impression that every value is eroding, everything is deteriorating, everything is growing more and more degraded. His smile indicates that he believes nothing can be done to resist or prevent this process. Silently, I reflect that perhaps the title of his second novel might serve as a kind of collective title for all his work: *Let It Come Down.*

Paul Bowles has been to us a most generous, courteous and considerate host. Whatever private terrors or obsessions he may keep in check beneath his impeccable dress and urbane manner may be guessed at from his fiction. Concerning the man, I have no insights to offer, only a few observations made on the basis of brief acquaintance. My impression of Bowles is that of a patient, tolerant, gracious man, who despite his fundamental pessimism and sense of futility endeavors to live according to a precise personal code, evincing fortitude, humor and a forbearing nature.

We sail back to Algeciras on the *Ibn Batouta,* leaving behind us the white city of Tangier. White gulls wheel behind the boat and a school of dolphins leaps in the sunlight. At last only the tower of the new mosque is visible and then that too is gone.

Postscript:

Many years later I was saddened to read in a piece in the *TLS* that Bowles and Mrabet had had a falling out and were bitterly estranged from each other. I don't know if they were ever reconciled.

Paul Bowles remained in Tangier until his death in late 1999. Mohamed Mrabet continues to live in Tangier. His artworks have been widely exhibited in Europe, the United States and North Africa and collections of his stories continue to appear in English and French translation.

Talking with the Man Who Let the Mice In: Two Visits to Brion Gysin

My first acquaintance with Brion Gysin came through reading "The Poem of Poems." The title is not a boast but a literal description of Gysin's twelve-page text, which blends together disjointed fragments of a number of pre-existing poems, including "The Song of Solomon," Shakespeare's sonnets, and T.S. Eliot's translation of "Anabasis" by St. John Perse. The product of this

process is a verbal collage, created not by physically cutting and re-arranging the source texts but by reading each text aloud into a tape recorder and then randomly mixing and re-mixing them again and again until they are thoroughly combined.

This audacious act of literary sacrilege appeared in *The International Literary Annual* for 1961.[1] Gysin's poem is shot through with enchantment and terror, whimsy and enigma: "the laugh of the dead in her blood... my heart twittered with joy under the quicklime... He moved his treasure through their door and my bowels were moved for him... the stale smell of morning overlaid with sapphire... silver fountains in the smoke of dreams."

Gysin had released a poetry latent in random, autonomous language, creating through incongruous juxtapositions of words new networks of conceptual correspondence.

Brion Gysin was also a painter, an inventor (of the Dream Machine, a device for flicker-induced hallucinations), an historian, a performance artist, the founder of a school of sound poetry, the originator of "the cut-up method" and of permutated poetry, a friend and collaborator of William Burroughs, a friend of Paul Bowles, and something of a legendary figure in avant-garde circles. A short biographical note in *Contemporary Artists* states that Gysin was an American citizen, born in Taplow, Buckinghamshire, England in 1916. He had lived in Paris in the 1930s and was associated with the surrealist group there, but had been expelled from the Surrealist movement by the express command of André Breton himself. Gysin traveled extensively in Europe and North Africa, pursued various occupations, including those of welder and restaurateur, and during World War II had served in both the U.S. and Canadian armies.[2] An inspiring life. The poet Gregory Corso once composed a short, cryptic, gnomic rhyme about him: "Brion Gysin let the mice in."

In November of 1979 I wrote a letter to Brion Gysin at his home in Paris, asking if my wife and I might call on him during our coming visit to that city. In reply, I received from him a color postcard of the Georges Pompidou Center on which Gysin had drawn with a marker two red arrows pointing to his apartment. On the reverse he had graciously written, "Hope to see you here in Paris. The red arrows point the way."

On the raw, wet evening of January 1st, 1980, Birgit and I took the small two-person elevator up to his 4th floor apartment and knocked on the door. Strange music came from within—horns braying, cymbals clashing. (This proved to be Tibetan ritual music.) We were admitted by Brion, shook hands and were introduced to his other guests that evening:

a young English writer named Terry Wilson, and Roberto, a young man from Brazil.

The living room clearly doubled as Brion's studio. There was an easel on which was mounted one of his calligraphic paintings and an improvised worktable with a desk lamp and a desk chair. A Moroccan ceramic ashtray and a blue hyacinth flower in a small purple pot occupied the table. Canvasses were stacked against the walls. At both ends of the room, books, magazines, LPs, and North African objects of brass or fired clay crowded the shelves. The books included Brion's own works, periodicals with his contributions, books on Islam, *The Tibetan Book of the Dead*, a book on Eleusis, *Raise Up Off Me* by Hampton Hawes, and novels by William S. Burroughs. A narrow hallway connecting the living room and bedroom was also stacked with canvasses and with Dream Machine cylinders. Brion's bed was just a mattress on the floor, surrounded by a gramophone, a tape recorder, tapes, and records. All through the evening music played: Tibetan, Moroccan, Spanish, Ornette Coleman.

Gysin himself was a tall man in his mid-sixties with thick gray hair and blue-green eyes. Light-complected with a rosy flush, his face was merry and lively (reminding me somewhat of the actor Walter Pigeon), though at times his physiognomy took on a hollow, hungry, bony, woeful aspect (reminding me somewhat of certain later photographs of Antonin Artaud). He was dressed in brown, flared corduroy pants, brown boots, a brown Moroccan vest worn over a collarless white shirt, and a dark brown cardigan. His speech sounded North American with occasional English pronunciations and expressions. (He attended Downside College in England, 1932-34). In conversation he casually blended levels of discourse, mingling obscenities, hip argot and academic speech. When reading or doing close work with his hands (i.e. rolling joints), he put on a pair of narrow gold-rimmed reading glasses.

Brion served tea and at first the conversation centered upon his years living in Tangier. He spoke with affectionate disapproval of his friend Paul Bowles, whom he considered somewhat crafty and artful. In the early 1950s Bowles had invited Gysin to share a house with him in the medina of Tangier. Heretofore, Gysin explained to us, the medina had been inhabited exclusively by Moroccans while Europeans lived in the European quarter of the city. Gysin saw himself in this regard as having been used as Bowles's "patsy," in that Bowles had bought the house intending only to use it by day as a studio where he could compose music and had not intended to *live* there. Brion, however, proceeded to move into the house on a permanent basis, occupying it day and night. In this way, Bowles had calculated that he could observe and gage the reactions of the neighbors and other inhabitants of the medina to this intrusion without endangering himself. Bowles, Brion said, did not mix socially with the Moroccans, did not smoke kif with them or frequent their cafés, as he himself did.

Jane Bowles, Brion said, he had found consistently and continually exasperating. Never had he met a woman so proficient at disrupting plans, so adept at stalling, sabotaging, derailing all manner of movement or action. Ah well, he said, *de mortuis nil nisi bonum.* (Of the dead, speak nothing but good.)

Gysin believed that the final scenes in Bowles's novel, *The Sheltering Sky,* in which the female protagonist, Kit, is kidnapped and confined in a house by an Arab man, derived from Bowles's own experiences in Morocco during the 1930s when he was once locked up in a house by his hosts. Bowles's blond hair and light complexion were much admired by Moroccan women, Gysin said, who sent their husbands to Bowles to inquire how he achieved his appearance. To their question Bowles had replied: "Carrots. I eat lots of carrots."

Brion recalled with fondness Dean's Bar in Tangier. Anthony Blunt, who had only recently been revealed as having been a Soviet spy, one of the Cambridge group, had frequented Dean's, he said. He surmised that at one time or another, "all that lot were there." It was a place, Gysin said, where spies, writers, underworld figures, exiles, expats and celebrities all mixed. Anyone might show up at any time. Strange to say, almost alone among all of the bar's many customers, William Burroughs had been unwelcome there. Dean had taken an immediate dislike to him and served him only with the greatest reluctance. As for Joseph Dean himself, the proprietor, he was something of a mystery. No one really knew him. He was rumored to be on the lam from some criminal act or scandal in his past. But then so, too, said Brion, were any number of other residents of Tangier.

Gysin spoke of his fascination with Moroccan trance cults and the ecstatic brotherhoods of Morocco. Their practices, he believed, went back to ancient tribal customs among the earliest inhabitants of the Tigris and Euphrates area, back perhaps all the way to the Biblical figure of Abraham, father of all Semites, an outcast to the marshlands of what is present day Iraq. He mentioned Flaubert's novel, *Salammbô,* as an astonishingly accurate account of the trance cults of North Africa and the Middle East. He was puzzled, he said, to know how Flaubert had acquired this knowledge. Gysin's own acquaintance with the Master Musicians of Joujouka had made him aware of their remarkable knowledge of events and family relations of many centuries past. They possessed a kind of unwritten tribal memory. It was they who had persuaded him to remain in Morocco and who had given him the idea for the restaurant that they had run together in Tangier for some years. Ultimately, though, some among them must apparently have resented his inquiries into their history and secrets and had laid a curse upon him. Hidden in a ventilation duct in the restaurant, a magical bundle had been discovered, a collection of objects such as seeds and stones and pieces of broken mirror together with a written spell designed to affect his departure. He had taken the hint, for on one previous occasion when he had been in a remote district of the Moroccan countryside in the company of two Moroccan men, exploring a cave, he had overheard one of them ask the other: "why don't we just kill this Rumi and take his shoes?" Accordingly, when the magic bundle had been discovered he had been inclined to act upon the warning. Gysin seemed to place a good deal of credence in the practice of magic, especially that of words and writing. He remarked that the Punic name of the god Pan was so powerful that it "would burn up the paper if written down."

At one point, perhaps at the request of Terry Wilson, our host produced a photo album containing photographs of Brion looking very fit in abbreviated bathing trunks, Brion in a djellaba, Brion wearing a fez, Brion shaved-headed, bearded, and clad in a kaftan, Brion with a round taqiyah cap on his head, Brion wearing a suit and tie. He seemed to be a man of many costumes, many faces. There were also photos of his friends John Latouche and Carl Van Vechten (and a fine photo of Brion taken by Van Vechten). Latouche, he said, had been a truly "mad cat," a highly talented song lyricist with a wild sense of humor. Gysin recalled that once he and Latouche and a few others had been riding together in a taxi cab in New York City collectively, spontaneously writing the lyrics to "Taking a Chance on Love." Gysin had provided the lines: "Here I slide again / about to take a ride again / starry-eyed again." Others in the taxi had contributed other lines. Latouche had had to buy from them their several contributions to the song or the copyrighting of the lyrics would have proven too complex. Carl Van Vechten had also been a good friend and an inspiration; a writer, critic and photographer instrumental in promoting black culture among white readers during the 1920s and '30s. The title of his novel, *Nigger Heaven,* had however "caused a good deal of pain to some very dear friends of mine" in the black community, Gysin said. Brion shared Van Vechten's passion for all things black, immersing himself in the music and street life of 52nd Street in New York City, and later writing a study of Josiah Henson, the man who provided the original model for Harriet Beecher Stowe's fictional figure of Uncle Tom. Gysin had also written a history of slavery in Canada.[3]

Also in Gysin's photo album were photographs of the Moroccan painter Mohamed Hamri, on whom Gysin had based the character of Hamid in his novel, *The Process*. Hamri, Gysin said, had discovered his vocation as an artist by decorating the interior of a brothel in Rabat, covering the walls with portraits and murals that had excited the admiration of the prostitutes and their clients. He was completely self-taught, self-invented, a natural genius, Gysin said, a painter with an innocent eye and the most paradisiacal vision since Paul Gauguin. And, Hamri was completely unspoiled spiritually by his success, often using his earnings to benefit his village and his extended family. Once when Hamri was a guest in the luxurious New York apartment of a wealthy collector and patroness of the arts, he had gestured dismissively to all her expensive, exquisite furnishings and possessions and had remarked: "The trouble with you, Madam, is that you think all of this is real." Gysin clearly endorsed this view of the material world.

Gysin's album also contained photos of his friend and collaborator, William S. Burroughs. There had been, Gysin said, an extraordinary photograph of Burroughs taken in his room at the Beat Hotel in which Burroughs sat under a bare light bulb smoking a cigarette with the smoke curling above his head forming shapes of demons, fiends, snakes and the faces of evil spirits. The photograph was unsettling to Burroughs and, indeed, it was so frightful to look at that it had been airbrushed – against the wishes of the photographer, Loomis Dean – before appearing uncredited in *Life* magazine.

Gysin spoke of his childhood in a small frontier town in western Canada, living with his widowed mother, (his father was killed in the battle of the Somme just months after Brion was born) and his stepfather, who was an Indian agent, growing up there in a Wild West ambiance of brawls, knifings, and shootings. At the age of fifteen he was sent to a boarding school in England where he felt ashamed at coming from such an uncouth, provincial background. He felt himself to be something of an outsider among his English classmates, many of whom came from "better families," and he had avoided as much as possible any mention to the other boys of his personal history. His mother, he said, could not afford to pay his fare to return home to Canada during the summer holidays. Indeed, when he set off for England he had traveled across Canada by cattle train and then across the Atlantic by cattle boat.

At the earliest opportunity he moved to Paris to pursue a career in art, arriving in 1934, and living there on a pittance. He mixed in surrealist circles and had been on the verge of exhibiting some of his work in a show of surrealist drawings when, only a day before the opening of the exhibit, André Breton ordered that Gysin's drawings be taken down and removed from the gallery. Gysin believed that the reason for his exclusion from the exhibit was Breton's virulent dislike of homosexuals. It was apparent that nearly fifty years later Gysin still felt aggrieved by this rejection, this humiliating and unreasonable deflection of his career. Even among outsiders such as the surrealists, he had been made to feel an outsider. In this regard, he took vindictive satisfaction in the indignities visited upon Salvador Dali and his wife just across the street at the Pompidou Center. Brion had witnessed the arrival of Dali in an expensive car and an outré costume for the opening of a major Dali retrospective. But the staff of the Pompidou Center had gone on strike, and when Dali made his pompous arrival, they booed and menaced him. Brion relished Dali's discomfiture, thinking that the preposterous old clown deserved it for his inexcusable public statements praising Franco and the Falangist regime and for enthusiastically supporting the execution of the Basque terrorists.

At present Brion was pursuing three projects, he said. He was working with the soprano saxophonist Steve Lacy, collaborating on an album of songs for which Brion was providing the texts. He was also engaged in writing a novel based on the life of the Beat Hotel. He showed us a large, carefully executed, minutely detailed pencil drawing depicting the spiral staircase, the floors, and individual rooms of the hotel. And, finally, he was once again hoping to market his Dream Machine. He presented us with a handsome brochure created by Carl Laszlo, Editions Panderma in Basel, Switzerland. It was essentially a prospectus for the Dream Machine written in German, French, and English, explaining the action, purpose, and effect of the device. I mentioned the 1962 issue of *Olympia* magazine that had included a do-it-yourself kit for building a Dream Machine.[4] "We tried to give it away, man, we couldn't even give it away," he lamented. "The Dream Machine should have been the drugless turn-on of the 60s," he said, but he had never succeeded in finding a financial backer to put the machine into production. He still harbored some hope of seeing it marketed properly, but after so much time and so many attempts he was more sanguine in his expectations.

He was also pessimistic about the current world situation, especially the Soviet invasion of Afghanistan that had only just taken place (i.e. in late December of 1979). "We've lost the Great Game," he lamented. The longstanding, grim, vital competition between East and West for control of Central Asia had now in one stroke been decisively won by the Russians. Moreover, the U.S.S.R. would soon control a corner of the Mediterranean and the Atlantic by taking over part or perhaps ultimately all of Morocco by means of their "Polisario fiction." The non-existent Polisario, he believed, were no more than a cat's paw for Russian expansion. He regretted that the United States was so ill-served by President Carter.

"Carter's redneck mentality," he said, "fulfils the worst fears and prophecies of H.L. Mencken." And as for the president's staff, his advisers, "what a rare batch of assholes!" He paused to correct himself: "No, not assholes. The asshole is a delectable thing. What a choice cluster of ninnies!"

For that matter, though, in his view things had been going downhill since the fall of the Roman Empire. It was not surprising to him that things had declined to their current state. As for his personal politics, he said, from the 1930s to the present: "I'm an observer. I'm not a joiner." The real human project, he said, should be to leave behind the material, temporal world and enter the eternal freedom of Space. Conflicting ideologies and interest groups (including feminists) were hindering this project. "You're never going to get to Space that way," he said.

In the course of the evening we consumed several litres of beer and several joints. Gysin rolled joints in a fashion I had witnessed in Morocco. First he stuck together two Job cigarette papers. He then split open one of his Player's cigarettes and spilled the tobacco into the two Job papers. From a small round box he sprinkled crumbled flakes of cannabis

on the tobacco, then rolled the papers tight. He also prepared for us an impromptu meal, created out of odds and ends he had on hand. He hadn't bothered to shop, he said. Standing in his narrow kitchen (he could reach both the sink and the stove simultaneously) he made a dish of sausages and mashed potatoes, together with a salad of lettuce and endives. It was delicious.

As we were leaving, Brion asked where we were staying. He was amused to hear that we were lodged at the old hotel at 9 rue Git-le-Coeur, no longer a nameless 13th-class establishment but now a two star hotel called Hotel du Vieux Paris. "A literary pilgrimage," I explained. He confessed that he had himself once done the same when he was younger, seeking out and staying at a particular hotel in Paris that figured in a strange novel by Somerset Maugham titled *A Christmas Holiday*.[5]

~

My second (and last) visit with Brion Gysin took place on the evening of December 29th, 1981. In the two-year interim, we had exchanged a few letters. I had telephoned him after our arrival in Paris asking if we might call on him again. He immediately extended an invitation. He could use some company, he said. In the past few days he had been experiencing "premonitory shortness of breath" and was feeling depressed. We arrived at the appointed hour, bearing half a dozen litres of beer. Gysin had a hacking cough and in the course of the evening suffered several seizures of coughing. The coughing and shortness of breath had shaken him, he said. In consequence, he had just given up smoking Player's cigarettes, a brand he'd smoked since he was seventeen years old. But he had not given up smoking tobacco altogether, merely switched to another brand of filter cigarette, hoping that doing so might serve to quell or help to assuage his cough.

He had recently traveled to New York City, he said, to promote his new LP titled *Songs*[6], the collaboration with Steve Lacy he'd been working on during our last visit. The record included some of his permutated poems and some song lyrics ("Nowhere Street") he had written as long ago as the late 1940s, when he had hoped to turn his book, *To Master a Long Goodnight,* into a musical. He and Lacy had been seeking a female singer to perform the songs, perhaps to take the repertoire on the road.

New York City had not been to his liking; he had found little there that was agreeable. In restaurants, the food portions were too large and the quality of the food rather poor. He remembered with fondness the pies he had enjoyed there in the 1940s and the tasty homemade relish then available at lunch counters. The political situation, too, had deteriorated markedly, he thought. He ridiculed a recent revealing blunder made by some official in the U.S. State Department who had meant to send a note of reproval to Mauritania and had instead sent it to Mauritius, apparently unaware of the difference between the two countries.

This level of ignorance and incompetence, he believed, was a consequence of a purge in the State Department that had taken place in the early 1950s, when numbers of well-educated and efficient homosexuals had suddenly been dismissed from their jobs. This purge had occurred, he said, because "a group of dykes had blown the whistle on them." (The event to which he was referring is known as "the Lavender Scare." It is quite true that in 1950 some scores of gay civil servants were, indeed, dismissed from their positions with the State Department after being labeled "security risks" because, as homosexuals, they were thought to be vulnerable to blackmail by Soviet agents. What Gysin may have meant by his remark concerning "dykes" informing on the male homosexuals remains uncertain.)

He viewed this event as ruinous and fateful. Small wonder, he said, that American foreign policy had for so long been in such disarray and that the State Department was now staffed with people who didn't know Mauritius from Mauritania.

He reminisced about Paris in the 1930s and the people he had met then. Once, in 1934, after drinking all through the night, he had gone to meet the painter Pavel Tchelichew arriving from London on the early morning boat train. Gysin had brought with him a taxi cab full of flowers to welcome Tchelichew, who strolled forth from the train with the handsome young Charles Henri Ford on his arm. This was how Brion had met Charles Henri. Later, Ford had shown himself to be a good friend: on one occasion Gysin admitted to him that he had no money at all to make it through the summer, and Ford immediately reached down to his penny-loafer and removed from it a folded hundred dollar bill, presenting it to Gysin as a gift. The hundred dollars had been hidden there to serve as Ford's "mad money," but he had unhesitatingly and generously given it to Gysin.

On another occasion a chance meeting in the streets of Paris had led to a strange adventure. It had happened that one day Gysin had encountered a corpulent man walking a boxer dog on a leash. The dog had immediately taken to Brion, demonstrating inordinate affection for him and in this manner Brion had become acquainted with the dog's owner, a man named Nat North. Nat believed that he knew the area in which the renowned Holy Grail of medieval Christian tradition might be hidden. His belief, based on research into various Rosicrucian, Templar, and Cathar traditions, was that Joseph of Arimathea had not brought the grail as far as England, but had instead deposited it near Montségur in southern France, near Andorra. Gysin's new friend enlisted his aid in attempting to locate the artifact.

Together, at Nat's expense, they traveled to Montségur where they spent some weeks exploring ancient caves associated with the Cathars. In one such cave, behind a crumbling stone wall, they found scores of skulls and piles of bones probably dating from the Albigensian Crusade. Nat, however, was being followed and persecuted by a Nazi agent who was in quest of the same object. Heinrich Himmler's agents had already secured the Spear of Longinus, said Gysin, and desired intensely to possess the Holy Grail. This Nazi agent had Nat North expelled from France, so that he and Brion never had time to complete their investigations.

In the meantime, Brion discovered that he was claustrophobic and could not endure any further cave exploration. But he believed that he may have discovered a likely location for the grail to have been hidden. He had come upon a cave in which elaborate and difficult labor had been undertaken to cover a large hole. There were also mason's marks visible on this construction. Brion felt there was a strong possibility that this particular place was the location of the Holy Grail, spirited away by a small group of Cathar knights while they were under siege. And now he alone knew where it was. The grail itself, he said, was not a chalice or cup but a simple paten carved out of a large emerald. Brion also informed me that when Nat North returned to New York he was educated as a medical doctor, later became a practicing psychoanalyst, was also a bullfight critic, and later danced the part of Silenus in a ballet. (Although Brion's tale sounds a bit far-fetched, it is true that Otto Rahn, an archaeologist and a member of the S.S., made two expeditions to Montségur in the 1930s, searching for the Holy Grail, and that Himmler himself later undertook a mission to the Monserrat Abbey in Spain in quest of the grail. Apparently, their belief was that possession of the grail would convey upon them and their cause supernatural powers.)

I asked him about his experiences during the war years and he said that in the early 1940s he had worked in New York City as a stage designer and as a welder in a shipyard, but in both instances rigid union regulations prevented him from continuing in these occupations. During that same time, he applied for American citizenship and had been drafted into the army. He underwent infantry training and then volunteered for the paratroopers. However, he broke his wrist on the very first tower jump and this injury put an end to his brief career with that elite unit. Partly in consequence of this disappointment and partly because he had still not obtained American citizenship, he determined to transfer to the Canadian army. Gysin described for us the strange, solemn, ceremonial scene of his formal transfer from the one national army to another. In a large room, together with a score or so of other soldiers from both armies who stood on either side of the room, he stood at attention on one side of a white line painted on the floor. There were soldiers transferring from the Canadian to the American army, and soldiers going the other way. Upon command, the soldiers stripped themselves of all their clothes, including their underclothes, stacking their uniforms behind them in a neat pile. Upon a second command, the now naked soldiers advanced across the white line (either to the north or to the south), and upon a third command, they dressed themselves in the uniform of the army to which they had transferred. In the Canadian army, he studied to be a Japanese interpreter, he said, learning to draw Japanese characters with brush and ink. It was also in the Canadian army that he met Tex Henson, the great-grandson of Josiah Henson, who was the inspiration for the title character of Harriet Beecher Stowe's novel, *Uncle Tom's Cabin*. Conversations with Tex inspired Gysin to research and write *To Master, a Long Goodnight*, subtitled *the story of Uncle Tom, a historical narrative.*

While in the American army, Gysin had designed an emblem that he then had tattooed on his left shoulder blade. It was to serve both as an individual identification mark and as a personal sign for luck or protection. With this unique emblem indelibly inscribed on his body, he felt that he formed "a club of one," he said. Years later, on a beach, Somerset Maugham had admired it and had subsequently had his current "catamite" so tattooed, Brion said. Gysin felt intense disapproval at this act of uninspired imitation. It was as if something that he felt bestowed upon him a certain power or protection had now been taken away from him by Maugham's presumptuous appropriation. By the way, he asked, had we read Anthony Burgess's novel, *Earthly Powers*? We had, we said. It was absolutely uncanny, Brion thought, how well Burgess had succeeded in capturing "the old man" (i.e. Maugham). Burgess did a splendid job, he thought, getting down Maugham's mannerisms, his attitude, his bearing, his speech, his aura, the very spit and image of him. Gysin found Burgess's fictional portrait truer to life than the biography of Maugham written by his own friend, Ted Morgan.

I asked Brion how his novel was progressing, the narrative based on the Beat Hotel. He had written seven chapters so far, he said. The hotel in his novel was called the Bardo Hotel (which was also his working title for the book) and comprised seven floors and a total of forty-nine rooms. The rooms would represent the forty-nine day state of intermediate existence following physical death, as described in the *Tibetan Book of the Dead.* The seven levels of the hotel would in his novel correspond to ascending levels of sexual experience, identity, and awareness. The posthumous experiences of the protagonist in the various rooms and at the various levels of the hotel would encompass memory, temptation, terror and catharsis, as in the Bardo state.

Beneath the Bardo Hotel flows a river based on the river Bièvre which, he said, does run beneath the streets of Paris and empties into the Seine. He said that as you cross the Pont d'Austerlitz walking south to the left bank you can sometimes see the river bubble up as it enters Seine water. Indeed, it is this long covered-over, underground river that gives the rue de Bièvre its name, he said. Printers there used to dump their broken type into the water and also used the river to pulp their pages (sometimes whole editions of unsold books) and wash away the printed ink, whereafter the pulped pages could be drained and dried and rolled to be reused for printing new pages and new books. In his novel, Gysin said, this underground river would serve as a metaphor for the river of language, the river of words, running hidden and secretly beneath all our structures, our lives, our consciousness. (Brion makes use of this image in his novel, *The Last Museum,* where he describes the river *Chie* flowing beneath the hotel as an alphabet soup awash with inky words bleached from the pages of old books, its waters bearing all the words in the world and all of human memory.[7] Gysin's name for the fictional river *Chie* derives from the French verb for evacuating the bowels.)

In the jargon of the French publishing trade, he said, the term for pulping an entire edition of a book that had failed to sell in sufficient numbers was derived from the name of the publisher-martyr Étienne Dolet. Dolet had been executed by the authorities of church and state for publishing a scandalous book and there was a monument to him on the Place Maubert, which was located at one end of the rue de Bièvre, thus in his novel the underground river flowed beneath this monument. The ghost of Dolet would be a presence in *Bardo Hotel*, Gysin said, a presiding spirit of the river of words, a ghost to be laid. (Étienne Dolet is mentioned in *The Last Museum* on page 76 and again on page 166 where an attempt is made to blow up his statue.)

To "rub out the word" was, of course, the ultimate goal of Gysin's writing and of all his work. Brion, who spoke several languages, saw language as imposing a reductive pattern on thought, circumscribing what can be conceived or experienced. Each language, he said, is constructed upon a system of implicit ideas and assumptions and so captures its speakers in a constructed version of reality. There was an historic link, he said, between grammar and monotheism, both were instruments of control, both were limitations, constraints. His writing was a challenge to these codifications of reality, an attempt to undermine them, to dismantle them, and thus to extend the range of vision into the unseen and the unknown.

He spoke with admiration of Eugen Herrigel's *Zen in the Art of Archery*.[8] The concept of transcending technical execution and conscious control through self-abandonment had been an inspiration for both his writing and his painting, he said. Employing this method, ordinary habits of perception could be overcome, new connections could be made. (By this time, much beer and not a few joints had been consumed. In addition, Brion had downed four large glasses of whiskey.) The world, Brion believed, was becoming increasingly regulated and standardized. Consider, he said, the standardization of time. Time zones that extended around the world had been established by western nations, imposing upon Asians, Arabs and Africans the western concept of time, notions of how it must be measured and how it should be used. Wasn't it Martin Luther who had equated time and money? he asked. There was now an orthodoxy of time, a single, authoritative definition ordained and decreed for all of humanity.

There was even an international date line. Like the advent of grammar and monotheism, he viewed universal prescriptive conventions of the measurement of time as false and artificial. Since time was itself a prison, the standardized measurement of time was a prison within a prison; it was a further impediment to liberation. I asked whether he was familiar with J.W. Dunne's curious book *An Experiment in Time*. He said that both he and William Burroughs had read and admired the book during their days at the Beat Hotel. Dunne's theory of serial time was at once too mathematical and too abstract, he said, but the author's accounts of his prophetic dreams were remarkable and were clearly constituted evidence of some kind of liberation from time.[9]

Woozy now, we wobbled from topic to topic. He spoke of his early childhood memories of living at home with his very proper mother. As a little boy he had been the only male among a household of females and he had hated it. One day there had been a visit by a handsome and charming young man to whom Brion was immediately attracted. This event had been for him like a revelation or an awakening. His stepfather, with whom they later lived, had been a retired colonel in the Canadian army, administrating an Indian Reservation. He believed that his stepfather was a homosexual who had married his mother for her money. Since World War II, Brion had seldom returned to Canada. Now the country was run by "pseudo-swingers" like the Trudeaus, whom he deplored, he said. He was particularly appalled by Margaret Trudeau, who had, he said, insulted his dear friend, the Moroccan painter Ahmed Yacoubi, and who had "betrayed the Rolling Stones." She had "fixed" Pierre Trudeau in the same way that Laura Riding had "fixed" Robert Graves.

The quality of American political leaders was no better, of course. He could not understand the reluctance of the current U.S. administration to provide arms and assistance to the Moroccan government in their struggle against the Polisario. If the U.S.S.R. (who had invented the Polisario) were to gain control of the Western Sahara and blast or dig a harbor there, they could have "North America under one gun and South America under another." It was all so sad and stupid, he said. He also complained bitterly of his own lack of literary and artistic success, of recognition, of money. His Dream Machine had failed in the marketplace; he felt marginalized, neglected, rejected.

All evening, despite intermittent paroxysms of coughing, Gysin smoked cigarette after cigarette, interspersed with a good number of joints. He mourned his own dependence on tobacco "in the face of all good sense," he said. At length he ran out of cigarettes altogether and searched his trash basket for butts and smoked those. When those had been consumed, we set forth into the chill December night to buy more. Brion limped a bit (the result of a motorcycle accident) and walked hunched as he howled great yawns into the cold air. I asked him if he ever heard from Terry Wilson and he replied, "Yeah, every minute." I thought by this he might mean that he was unhappily in love with him or missing him acutely, so I didn't pursue the topic.

We parted ways shortly after. He invited us to call on him again.

~

Over the next few years we continued to exchange letters. Brion's cough proved to be emphysema, from which he died in 1986. Before his death he completed a final, monumental painting, which many critics consider to be his culminating work: "Calligraffiti of Fire."

In what sense can it be said that "Brion Gysin let the mice in?" How should we understand Gregory Corso's cryptic little poem? Letting the mice in—an unconventional, unhygienic action—is the act of an insurrectionist, a subversive, one who aims to undermine and defeat established practices. The common denominator of Gysin's painting, his writing, his sound poems, and his Dream Machine is to overturn ordinary habits of perception, to overthrow traditional ways of meaning, and to allow unperceived, unknown realities to enter our consciousness. Gysin was in league with those primal energies that oppose systems, categories, orthodoxies, dogma, conventions, habits of being, and habits of seeing. Brion Gysin "let the mice in" because he believed that art exists to transform the human eye and mind.

Just as Gysin's "The Poem of Poems" mixes disparate texts to create a new poetic work, so too, the beliefs, concepts, and attitudes that comprise his personal artistic credo combine elements from various sources to create new modes of vision and expression. There is in the complex of ideas and impulses from which his work springs a quantum of Rimbaudian romanticism, another of romantic primitivism, a dash of Dada, a generous portion of surrealist sensibility, a dollop of non-linear writing after the manner of Gertrude Stein, and a measure of Moroccan magic, all mixed with elements of western scientific thought.

In truth, I can't say that I shared many beliefs or opinions with Brion. Iconoclasm and heresy can all too often and too easily become categorical imperatives and become in their own right forms of orthodoxy. At a personal level, his occasional vainglory and vituperation and misogyny could be painful to bear. But I honor the essential yearning for mystery and transcendence that informs his oeuvre, and the urgency and evocative power of his best work. Despite the retrospective exhibitions that have been organized since his death, and despite the publication of an anthology of his writing, his reputation and position remain uncertain.[10] Even posthumously, he continues to hover at the margins of many movements, groups, and schools, ultimately inassimilable to any, a perpetual dissident.

Notes

1. "The Poem of Poems" by Brion Gysin in *International Literary Annual,* edited by Arthur Boyars and Pamela Lyon. London: John Calder, 1961, pp. 75-86.

2. *Contemporary Artists.* New York: St. Martin's Press, 1977, pp. 374-375.

3. *To Master, A Long Goodnight. The Story of Uncle Tom, A Historical Narrative,* with "The History of Slavery in Canada" by Brion Gysin. New York: Creative Age Press, 1946.

4. "Dream Machine" by Brion Gysin in *Olympia,* No. 2, 1962, pp. 31-32.

5. *Christmas Holiday* by W. Somerset Maugham. London: William Heinemann, 1939.

6. *Songs* by Steve Lacy and Brion Gysin. Recorded on January 28 and 29, 1981 in Paris, France. Vinyl 12 inch LP and 7 inch EP in box set. Released by Hat Hut: Switzerland, 1981.

7. *The Last Museum* by Brion Gysin, London: Faber & Faber, 1986, pp. 75-77.

8. *Zen in the Art of Archery* by Eugen Herrigel. New York: Pantheon Books, 1953.

9. *An Experiment in Time* by J.W. Dunne. London: Faber & Faber, 1927.

10. "Brion Gysin: I Am That I Am" curated by Bruce Grenville and José Férez Kuri at The Edmonton Art Gallery, 1998. "Brion Gysin: Dream Machine" curated by Laura Hoptman at the New Museum of Contemporary Art, New York, 2010. *Back in No Time: The Brion Gysin Reader* edited by Jason Weiss. Wesleyan University Press: Middletown, CT: 2001.

A Glimpse of Robert Graves
Deyá, Majorca, 1978

It was unmistakably him. Tall, rugged and husky, with pale blue-gray eyes fixed on me. Bent nose, a storm of gray curls beneath a black broad-brimmed, flat-crowned Spanish hat. Robert Graves! For years I had dreamed of this moment and had travelled far in hope of such an encounter. Now the instant and the event seemed unreal. In awe and trepidation I approached and introduced myself. "Yes," he said, "I know you."

Robert Graves first intersected my life in 1965 during my senior year in high school when I came across his poem "Rocky Acres" in the textbook for my English class. Deeply intrigued by this poem, I sought out his work at the Phoenix Public Library, from which I then borrowed his *Collected Poems.* Enjoying and admiring this collection, I soon bought a copy of the book. Over the next decade I bought and read everything by Graves that I could find: his poetry, his novels, his short fiction, his essays, his autobiography, his literary criticism.

A primary reason for my attraction to Robert Graves' writing was the appeal to me of the "romantic primitivism" that informed it. Graves seemed to me to embody a heroic opposition to scientific materialism and to the bleak aridity and dead end desolation of so much contemporary philosophy and literature. Here was a man who had been badly wounded – nearly extinguished – by the agencies of mechanistic industrial civilization. Here was a man who had been psychologically shattered by the dehumanizing, destructive horror of the forces of Modernity and who had found renewal and a sense of the sacred in primal mystery and archaic myth. In this sense, Graves was for me exemplary, a model and an ideal.

In 1972 I moved from Arizona to Denmark. Now I lived in the same time zone as Robert Graves in his stone house on the distant island of Majorca. Many mornings before going to work I drank my tea thinking of him, wondering what he might be doing at that early hour. Many nights I sat up late, smoking home grown marijuana and reading his books. It was not until 1978 that I was earning enough money to think of making the journey to Majorca and calling on him.

I would, of course, not call upon him unannounced. I would not for the world wish to intrude upon his privacy. I determined a course of action: I would send a message to his house via a local inhabitant of the little village where he lived, informing him that I would like to meet him but that I would entirely understand if he did not care to receive visitors.

And in the event that I did meet Robert Graves, what did I wish to happen? What did I expect? That he would impart to me some secret sacred knowledge or ancient wisdom? That he would immediately recognize in me a man of notable endowments and capacities? That I would, as they say, bathe in reflected glory? Or was it that as an earnest, eager Arizona provincial I just wanted to have me a looksee?

In late June of 1978, my wife, Birgit, and I travelled from our home in Odense, Denmark to Majorca, taking a night train from Odense to Copenhagen, a bus to Kastrup Airport, and a flight above the Alps and the Mediterranean to Palma de Majorca. From there we took a bus to Sóller on the northwest of the island, and from Sóller we took a taxi along a narrow winding coastal road to the village of Deyá. We found a room at the Pension Miramar, located on a hillside overlooking the village.

There was something enchanting, even magical, about Deyá. The village, situated on and around a hill, is surrounded by mountains on three sides with the sea to the north. Between the mountains and the village are terraced hillsides planted with almond trees and olive trees. You hear cocks crowing, the tinkle and jangle of sheep's bells, their bleating calls and someone playing a flute. At the top of the hill – called Es Puig – stands the Églésia de Saint Joan Baptista and the village cemetery. On the slopes of Es Puig, among the village houses, grow pines and cypresses, palm trees and cacti, oleander and hollyhocks.

The streets of Deyá are narrow, curving, steep and cobbled, the houses made of tan stone with terracotta tile roofs, green-shuttered and bright with bougainvillea. Embedded in walls at intervals along the streets are colored ceramic tiles depicting the Stations of the Cross and there is a stone fountain with a chained metal cup above which there are colored tiles portraying Christ as shepherd. There are a few small shops and a couple of cafés. To reach the Cala, a small shingle beach, you descend past houses, through olive groves, along a creek, over stiles, across stepping stones, down a dirt path and a rocky road (all the while from somewhere faraway a flute playing). There you can swim in the clear, cool Mediterranean water or eat at a terrace restaurant run by a fisher family while old fishermen sit nearby on wooden boxes mending their nets. It was soon clear to me why Graves had chosen this remote, serene village in which to pursue a life of authenticity and simplicity.

There was a small bookshop in the village run by an elderly Englishwoman. I bought a book from her and asked her how I might politely, tactfully get in touch with Robert Graves, explaining that we had no wish to impose ourselves on him or his family. "Oh, the Graves are very pleased to have visitors," she told me. "You would be very welcome at their house. They enjoy company." She assured me that there would be no need to ask permission or to communicate with the Graves beforehand. We should simply call upon them one afternoon.

The Graves' house was referred to as Canelluñ and was located about a mile out of the village on the road to Sóller. Robert Graves, she cautioned me, was no longer quite himself. His memory was much impaired, she said.

Bearing with us the gifts that we had brought from Denmark together with my copy of Graves' *Collected Poems,* in the bright heat of afternoon Birgit and I walked to Canelluñ. The two story stone house (built by Robert Graves and Laura Riding in the early 1930s) was set back from the road. We entered by way of an iron gate into a large garden. As we began to walk nervously toward the house, suddenly at a short distance from us we saw facing us three figures – a man and two women.

I recognized Robert Graves immediately. We stopped in our tracks, stammering our apologies and assurances that we did not mean to intrude or to impose ourselves. It was perfectly fine, one of the women said. We were welcome. We advanced and introduced ourselves. The slightly older of the two women was Beryl Graves, the poet's wife. The slightly younger of the two was Catherine Dalton, Graves' daughter by his first marriage. I was, of course, not a little surprised by Graves' claim to know me. I understood, however, that he was not referring to some mystical affinity between us, but that this misconception on his part must be due to his mental condition, of which the English lady in the book shop had informed me.

Very graciously, Beryl Graves invited us into the house. The interior was dim and cool. The walls were white-washed, the floors laid with smooth, yellow, stone tiles, the rooms furnished with antique brown wooden tables, chairs and cabinets. There were several handsome cats and a white poodle. I was surprised to see a television and a copy of *Time* magazine; unsurprised to see a lunar calendar. We were offered and accepted cold beer. Where did we come from? we were asked. When Birgit replied that she was from Odense, Denmark, best known, she said, as the birthplace of Hans Christian Andersen, Robert Graves exclaimed "bravo!" and clinked his glass with hers.

The gifts we had brought with us from Denmark were received with pleasure and interest. These included almond soap, black tea steeped in the juice of black currants, a bottle of Danish mead, and a jar of heather honey. We had also brought two pocket-size leather bound notebooks for Graves. When I offered them to him, though, he very courteously, very considerately indicated to me that I should have them. Later, however, when his wife placed the notebooks on the table, he reached for one and placed it in his shirt pocket. It was apparent by now that Graves was incapable of coherent conversation. He would begin a sentence and then stop abruptly, unable to find the next word. Or his remarks would be logically consistent enough in themselves ("You're going to be fine") but quite irrelevant to the topic at hand. Yet, he seemed withal very interested, very friendly. He observed to his wife and daughter: "It's been a long while since we've had such good people here." Addressing us, he said: "You're very decent people." And to Birgit he said: "You're a good woman."

We were told that in two days Robert and Beryl were leaving for London to stay there for a few weeks. Since when we arrived the two women had been about to take Graves for a walk in the garden, it was suggested that we accompany them. The five of us made a tour of the ample and fertile grounds surrounding the house, Beryl pointing out the various kinds of fruit trees, plants and vegetables planted in their large garden. There were carob trees, almond trees, orange trees, figs, cherries, apples, peaches and plums, apricots and grapes, green beans, potatoes, tomatoes, squash and lettuce, all grown by irrigation. They produced all their own vegetables, I was told, though they also shopped for certain items at a Supermarket in Palma. Beryl plucked ripe fruits from the trees and gave them to us, together with a bag of unshelled almonds. I remarked at one point on the beauty of their household cats and the cats I'd seen in the streets of the village. Beryl agreed and said that the cats I had seen were mostly descendants of their own Abyssinian cats brought by them to Deyá from England years ago.

When we returned to the house, I asked Beryl if she thought that Mr. Graves would be willing to sign a book that I had brought with me. She replied that she thought he might only be able to sign his name. I produced my copy of the *Collected Poems* and Beryl handed it to Graves, asking him if he could sign his name. "Of course, I can," he said, "do you take me for a fool?" Graves signed his name on the free end paper, dated his signature (the date being provided to him by Beryl) and then asked me my name, even inquiring if my last name were spelled with a "ph". After this we took our leave, Graves clasping my hand firmly and warmly and saying "Thank you for everything." We said goodbyes to Catherine and to Beryl, thanking them for receiving us. Beryl, seeing us out, said that she was only sorry that we should have found her husband so "very ill."

A second and final encounter with Robert Graves took place the following afternoon in a small café in the village. I entered the café and saw Graves and Catherine seated at a table. Catherine greeted me and motioned to me to sit with them. As we drank tea together, she recounted to me strange stories concerning her late husband, George Clifford Dalton, an atomic physicist from New Zealand. According to Catherine, her husband had been persecuted and ultimately poisoned by an international conspiracy including the Australian Secret Intelligence Service. Occasionally, Graves muttered a comment that I could not quite catch due to the level of noise in the café. After a time, Catherine left the table for a few minutes and Graves turned to me, making eye-contact, and with some urgency said to me: "It's all like this, you see." As he spoke, he extended his right index finger and with it described a circular motion (not pointed upward but rather with the back of the finger toward me). Uncomprehending, I nodded. I wondered afterward if he meant to tell me that all was awhirl within his brain or to communicate something else, some deeper truth or insight (the cyclical pattern of life or of history, the circle of eternity? who can say?) Before leaving the café, he shook my hand firmly and warmly and said: "God bless you."

During our remaining days in Deyá, we met the parish priest, Father Pedro, a very friendly man who, speaking to us in a mixture of English and German, kindly showed us the treasures of his church: a jewelled silver crucifix, a silver chalice and censer, all of them hundreds of years old. He had been priest of the Églésia de San Joan Baptista for 29 years, he said, and was well acquainted with Robert Graves. Señor Graves (*Grah-vés* as the good priest pronounced it) had unfortunately grown very absent minded in recent years, even sometimes misplacing his false teeth when he went for a swim at the Cala. Father Pedro was himself from Valldemossa, a nearby village where could be seen, he said, "many intelligent things," including a statue of St. Sebastian. We also met Martin Tallents, an English resident of the village and a close friend of Robert Graves. Martin invited us to his home for tea, showing us books he had received as gifts from Graves. As to Graves' current mental condition, he said that the poet still had occasional lucid intervals. Indeed, only a few days since, Graves had remarked to him: "It's curious, isn't it? I don't know if I'm alive or dead." Martin also entertained us with songs from a musical called "Marmalade" that he had recently written.

Together with Martin Tallents, we were invited by Catherine to dinner at Canelluñ. Beryl and Robert Graves had left for London a few days earlier. Catherine said that she had spoken to them by telephone and Beryl had related that she and Robert had seen the film of "The Shout," (based on Robert Graves' short story of the same name) and that Graves had seemed to recognize the dramatization of his story on the screen.

I asked if I might see Graves' study and was given permission to do so. The room, at the far end of the house, was furnished with a wooden desk and chair, a large wooden chest, and bookshelves. There were volumes by Laura Riding, John Crowe Ransom, e.e. cummings, Gertrude Stein, Alan Sillitoe, Siegfried Sassoon and Wilfred Owen. There was a copy of the *I Ching* and a shelf of books by and about T.E. Lawrence. There were volumes of Aeschylus, Sophocles, Euripides, Aristophanes, Ovid and Seneca. On the desk was a collapsible, folding lectern made of brass. On surfaces throughout the room were figurines and talismans, ancient relics, sea shells, fossils, coins and bones. On the walls were prints and paintings. There was a framed photograph of Graves' muse Julia Simon, together with a poem written by her. How strange it was to stand in this quiet room where words had been written that I had read in rooms so far away.

Dinner consisted of roast chicken, garden vegetables, a salad and red wine. Catherine held forth about sinister, incomprehensible intrigues, conspiracies, blackmail and murder, all undertaken by the Australian secret intelligence service with assistance from other intelligence services. She believed that the cause of her father's current mental condition was datura poisoning, undertaken against him for nefarious reasons. I asked when the loss of memory with which he was currently afflicted had first begun to manifest itself. Both Catherine and Martin reckoned that a certain loss of short-term memory had begun already sometime in the mid 1960s but had only become conspicuous by about 1972. A few years later, Graves' conversation had become increasingly less coherent. His decline had been a long, slow process. Clarity had alternated with confusion. There had been episodes in England and elsewhere abroad when Graves had wandered off alone and gotten lost in the streets. Even here in Deyá, he had on several occasions lost his way. He had ceased altogether to write poetry about three years ago.

At intervals as we ate dinner, one or another of the house cats would leap from the floor onto the table and make for the food on our plates. It was clear that they were accustomed to being indulged in this behaviour. Once I took one of them onto my lap and petted her. She purred for a time then suddenly bit and scratched me and ran away. A veritable "White Goddess" cat, I thought, sovereign, self-willed, capricious, cruel. I wondered if that was why the cats of Canelluñ were thus indulged.

While Martin and I washed the dinner dishes in the kitchen (where upon a shelf stood *Let's Eat Right* by Adele Davis) I asked him how Beryl had responded to her husband's devotion to a succession of muses. For the most part, Martin said, Beryl had borne these episodes very well, knowing that such passions and fixations were fleeting, necessary for Graves' work as a poet, and were not a threat to their marriage. Most of the muses had been discrete and decorous. The best and kindest, Martin thought, had been Julia Simon, whose photo I had seen on the wall of Graves' study. The most calamitous had been a wild young woman who called herself alternately Cindy or Emile. She had incarnated the muse in her baleful aspect and her influence upon Graves had been unfortunate. Martin said that during that time, he had twice witnessed Beryl weeping, though she had rushed out of the room to hide her tears. But concerning this recurrent compulsion of her husband to focus amorous reverence upon certain women, Beryl had once remarked to Martin that she had made her bed and now must lie in it. There were now, as might be expected, no further muses. And, of course, no further poems.

We left Canelluñ in the dark. Above the trees there was a waning crescent moon. It seemed a fitting valedictory sign for the end of our sojourn in the domain of the poet Robert Graves.

Name upon Name:
Encountering Pauline Réage/
Dominique Aury/Anne Desclos

"Through me forbidden voices, voices of sexes
and lusts, voices veil'd and I remove the veil."
—Walt Whitman

The pornographic paperback with an incongruously chaste white cover had been circulating around the barracks for some weeks before the now creased and curling copy came into my hands. Up to this time of my young life, the only explicit erotic writing that I had read was the thick Grove Press paperback of *My Life and Loves* by Frank Harris and that was all roguish and rollicking and jolly. This book was something altogether different. This was stern and severe, stark and solemn. And hauntingly strange.

The year was 1967, the place was Fort McClellan, Alabama; I was twenty years old, and the book was *Story of O* by Pauline Réage.[1] I read it with intense interest but little real attention, ignoring altogether the learned prefaces by Jean Paulhan and André Pieyre de Mandiargues. Yet even the most casual reader must ultimately find himself implicated in the paradoxes and ambiguities of this unsettling novel. For here is a story with its well-springs in the deepest recesses of consciousness, those William James named "the darker, blinder strata of character;" a story revelatory of the mystery, the power and peril of the erotic appetite. I was, to be sure, intrigued by the book, aroused and even discomposed while reading it, but – having once finished it and quickly going on to read *I, Jan Cremer,* another sexy Grove Press publication – I thought little more about it, except to feel a kind of lingering low-key awe.

A dozen years after this first encounter with *Story of O,* while browsing in a second-hand bookshop in Denmark, I came across and bought a used copy of the novel. (The same sedate Grove Press paperback edition bound in white covers.) I had at this time only recently read Susan Sontag's brilliant essay on "The Pornographic Imagination," and inspired by Sontag's insights, on this occasion I read *Story of O* more slowly and more thoughtfully.

This time I noted the absence of the definitive article in the title. Obvious, of course, but I hadn't taken note of it before or considered its implications. The provisionality of narrative that this deliberate omission suggests is further supported by the alternate beginnings and endings of the novel. I also remarked that although at the outset and throughout nearly all of the novel, an anonymous third person narrator relates the events of the story, maintaining a single character focus (we are told what O thinks and feels, but are not privy to the minds and emotions of other figures in the novel) this authoritative, impersonal, objective voice is not absolute or entirely consistent.

Curiously, for a few pages at one point of the novel the third person narrator becomes an uncertain first person narrator. This narrator's account is characterized by a self-conscious lack of precision. This narrator states that "they left her for half an hour, or an hour, or two hours, I can't be sure, but it seemed forever" (6) Then, with more conviction, the first person narrator declares "I know it was at this point . . .," (6) but soon thereafter admits that "I have no idea how long how long she remained in the red bedroom, or whether she was really alone, as she surmised" (7). The narrator then further acknowledges limitations to her or his complete knowledge of the events avowing "All I know is that when the two women returned, one was carrying a dressmaker's tape measure and the other a basket" (7) At this point, the first person narrator merges with the third person narrator and never again speaks as a separate voice. These uncustomary, incongruent elements in the text combine to make the novel strangely tentative and to lend it an oddly oneiric quality.

An attentive reading of *Story of O* reveals a resonant, poetic story written with scrupulous restraint. The central theme of the novel is the psychological transformation of the protagonist, O. Originally (anterior to the unfolding events of the story) a selfish, detached temptress, she becomes—through a series of self-willed ordeals—first a selfless lover, and finally a sacred figure. Accompanying O's inward transformation is a seasonal progression from the opening scenes of the novel, which take place upon a rainy autumn dusk to the final scene which takes place upon a clear summer dawn. O is also closely associated in the novel with the waning and waxing, obscurity and clarity of the moon. On the night of her arrival at Roissy, for example, we are told that "the moon raced high among the clouds," (7) while on the night of her final apotheosis at a villa in the south of France, we are informed that "the moon was almost full" (196) and that its bright light "fell full upon O" (197).

The poles of *Story of O* are those of the daylight world and the nocturnal world. The day world in the novel is that of familiar, quotidian reality, a realm of jobs, offices, apartments, furniture, clothes, tea, plants, restaurants, city streets, the weather, even cinemas and ice-cream. The nocturnal world is one of clandestine obsession and solemn ceremony, of instruments of restraint and torture, of willing submission to extremes of pain and humiliation, and of the relentless pursuit of ecstatic self-annihilation.

Appropriately, the story begins at dusk, a time of transition between day and night, just as O is about to undertake her own transition from the one realm to the other, from the familiar to the forbidden. O's goal is to surrender to the imperatives of the night domain to such a degree as to overthrow in her mind and spirit the daylight world. She desires to cast it off and repudiate it utterly, allowing the night world to invade and subdue the day, and ultimately to obliterate it altogether. This is the aim that with fear and anticipation O contemplates as she enters ever deeper and more definitively into the nocturnal world: "henceforth the reality of the night and the reality of day would be one and the same. Henceforth—and O was thinking, at last" (108).

O's determination in advancing toward her goal of carnal martyrdom is not, however, without a degree of ambivalence that causes her occasionally to balk, to regret and resist. It is as if there were within O two contending voices, the one impersonal, purposive and certain, the other wary and wavering. The division of O's will can be seen to be exteriorized in the novel's recurrent imagery of mirrors, and is perhaps also reflected in the brief, curious intrusion of a first person narrator, as noted above.

In the end, of course, it is O's resolute, impersonal will that wins and O fulfills entirely the course foretokened by her portentous name, becoming a cipher, open, empty, yet sacred and set apart, attaining the state of one who has died to a profane daylight sensibility and been reborn as an incarnation of mysterious primordial forces. Just as the name O may be seen to express emptiness, it may also be seen to symbolize a having come full circle, the achievement of completion, fulfillment.

That O is engaged in a quest for the absolute is reinforced by recurrent religious imagery in the text. The painful instruments of her self-transcendence are characterized as "blessed" (47); a submissive posture she must assume is likened to "the manner of the Carmelites" (55); and in her humiliations and sufferings she is "touched with grace" (94). These are to name but a few such instances. O may be seen as a species of inverted saint, one who through sexual surrender and abasement has willed the negation of her will and identity, one whose aim is self-extinction.

The strange, mythic quality of *Story of O* was until recently augmented by the secret nature of the author's identity, hidden by the pseudonym Pauline Réage. The "Translator's Note" appended to the Grove Press edition of the novel states that "To this day, no one knows who Pauline Réage is." (xi)

Similarly, in Susan Sontag's essay on "The Pornographic Imagination," Sontag remarks that "The real identity of Pauline Réage remains one of the few well-kept secrets in contemporary letters."[2] There was, inevitably, much speculation as to the identity of the author of this notorious book. Many critics were inclined to believe that despite the feminine pseudonym, the author was a man. Given the quality of the writing, names such as Jean Paulhan, André Pieyre de Mandiargues, André Malraux, Henri de Montherlant and Raymond Queneau were all put forward as being probable candidates for the real author behind the pseudonym of Pauline Réage.

On the basis of the text alone, what inferences can be drawn concerning the anonymous author of *Story of O*? The many precise details of dress and cosmetics, together with frequent references to flowers, would seem to suggest a female author, although admittedly such evidence in itself is in no way conclusive. The author would appear to be a person of education and culture. This is indicated not only by the understated elegance of the prose, but also by allusions in the text to Jonathan Swift (92), Leo Tolstoy (128) and *The Arabian Nights* (181), and to the painter Jean Antoine Watteau (167). Culture and education are further indicated by the narrator's knowledge of historical styles of costume, architecture, sculpture and furnishings. With regard to the latter, for example, the narrator can clearly recognize the characteristics of a "Restoration mirror" (110) and a "Regency bureau" (177).

Another inference concerning the pseudonymous author of *Story of O* that may be drawn from the text is that, in all likelihood, the author speaks

English. While today among French writers and intellectuals this ability may not seem remarkable, at the time of the publication of *Story of O* proficiency in English was an uncommon skill. I base this inference of English proficiency on the frequent occurrence in the text of conversations in English between O and Sir Stephen.

There is no indication in these exchanges that O is less than fluent in her command of English. Indeed, she even understands the trace of ambiguity implied in Sir Stephen's statement that iron becomes her, and later following a conversation with him, O reflects upon the coarseness of the English language where erotic matters are concerned. O also recalls having spent two months in Wales as child where a vivid impression was made upon her by a Biblical inscription (in English) painted on the wall of her room. Further evidence of the author's proficiency in English may be seen in the "Translator's Note" which precedes the text in the Grove Edition of *Story of O*. Here, the translator notes with some pride that through an intermediary, "the author has gone out of her way to say how pleased she is with those portions of the translation she has read." (xi)

However, having derived these conclusions or surmises from the text, I gave the matter of the real identity of Pauline Réage no further thought until a day in early January of 1980 when in a bin of books on sale at reduced prices outside a bookshop on the rue St. André des Arts in Paris, I found and bought a copy of a book titled *O m'as dit* by Régine Deforges.[3] Published in 1975, the book consists of a series of interviews conducted by Ms. Deforges with the author of *Story of O*. At the outset, the book confirms that Pauline Réage is, indeed, a woman.

The topics discussed during the interviews are many, including eroticism, love, religion, war and literature. Pauline Réage is both candid and expansive in her replies to questions put to her but scrupulously avoids providing specific facts such as names and places, information that might compromise her family and friends (*"pour ne gener personne"* as she says on page 167) or, indeed, serve to reveal her real identity. It is clear from her replies that Ms. Réage is very well read in literature and on a variety of other topics. She admits to having studied the history of costume and to having a passion for all that is English, characterizing herself as "an anglomaniac" (38).

In the course of the interviews she employs English words and phrases, cites English maxims, alludes to English authors and expresses a decided preference for the King James translation of the Bible. I could only discover in the interviews one specific bit of personal information that might be useful in establishing the true identity of the pseudonymous author, and that is the year of her birth. At one point, discussing her father's military service in the First World War, she states (131) that in the year 1914 she was seven years old, later (148) confirming her birth year stating that in 1917 she was ten years of age.

Among the few female names sometimes cited by critics or commentators as a possible real life identity behind the nom de plume of Pauline Réage (most often supposed to be a man) was the name of Dominique Aury. I was utterly unfamiliar with Dominique Aury but since her name was a kind of common denominator among the various speculations concerning Pauline Réage, I decided to determine whether any of the personal information that could be gleaned from the novel itself or from the interviews might correspond to her life and career. Accordingly, at the library I consulted a *Dictionaire Biographique* and read with interest the entry on Dominique Aury.

I learned that this name was itself a pseudonym for a French editor and literary critic whose real name was Anne Desclos. I noted that she was born in 1907. Also pertinent to my inquiry was the information that Dominique Aury had received a Licentiate degree in English and had translated from English to French numerous English and American novels. Moreover, she had also studied at the École de Louvre, which might account for Pauline Réage's acquaintance with the history of costume and knowledge of architecture and styles of household furnishings. I now felt reasonably certain that Dominique Aury (Anne Desclos) was the author of *Story of O.*

To acquaint myself with Madame Aury's writings, I read a collection of her literary essays, *Lectures pour Tous,* or as the book is titled in English, *Literary Landfalls.*[4] There are clear thematic correspondences between the essays collected in *Literary Landfalls* and *Story of O.* Both books celebrate passionate, obsessional, self-annihilating love. Aury's essay on the writer and theologian, Francois Fénelon, treats with sympathy his concept of Pure Love, "the soul abandoned to God" (18) in perfect obedience and in complete surrender to suffering even unto "death to self" (21). Aury expresses her admiration for the courage necessary to undertake such an uncompromising commitment; "to go with one's fate, to reject nothing, surrender oneself to the last" (22). (Pursuant to Aury's essay on Fénelon is the not altogether insignificant biographical sidenote that as a young student she attended the Lycée Fénelon.)

The very title of Aury's essay on the writings of Alfred de Vigny—"Obedience and Death"—resonates with *Story of O.* The ethos that informs Vigny's writings may be seen to represent for Aury a military counterpart to Fénelon's mysticism. "Man loves obedience," she observes, "which delivers him from himself, because secretly he loves not to belong to himself, he loves to lose himself" (64). And in a spirit clearly akin to that of *Story of O,* Aury writes approvingly, indeed longingly, of the "fascinating existence of a universe apart from the everyday universe... where the result of formal servitude is inner freedom" (65).

Writing of *Letters of a Portuguese Nun* (1669), Aury is moved by the book's eloquent expression of the ardent love of a young nun for a French cavalry officer. Such passionate, overmastering love, characterized by Aury as "the total possession of one person by another, without any sense, reason or justice" (75) can be seen to correspond to the unreserved, unrestrained love of O for René and later for Sir Stephen. Finally, among the essays, there is a comment on the nature of writing, which might well be taken as an expression of the author's own experiences with regard to her pseudonymous clandestine masterpiece of erotic fiction: "Whoever ventures to write betrays himself. You think you are saying one thing and you are admitting another. You disguise things and speak more truly than you know. The very disguise betrays you" (155).

The presence of so many significant and suggestive parallels between the literary essays of Dominique Aury and the themes expressed in *Story of O* convinced me that in all likelihood Madame Aury was the author behind the pseudonym of Pauline Réage.

One sad summer night in Tempe, Arizona as I walked under the stars and the streetlamps to my lonely job as a janitor, I was struck with the idea of writing a letter to the author of *Story of O*. About a month later— in September of 1980—I sent a birthday card written in French addressed to Anne Desclos (I can't now recall why I thought this name was more appropriate than Dominique Aury) at Éditions Gallimard in faraway Paris. Three months passed and then to my elation I received a reply. A note written in French in blue ink on *Nouvelle Revue Française* stationery thanked me for my friendly attention and for the (Japanese) card I had sent her, which she thought so beautiful that she had mounted it on the interior of a shelf above her bed where she could admire it.

Over the next thirteen years we corresponded intermittently, mostly between Denmark (to which I had returned) and France. For some reason unclear to me now, I persisted in addressing my early correspondence to Anne Desclos and she, in turn, signed her correspondence to me with that name. It was only in her third letter to me that she signed herself first as Anne Desclos and then as Dominique Aury, adding *"comme je m'appelle aussi, maintenant."* Subsequently, I addressed her by that nom-de-plume.

In response to my occasional cards and letters to Dominique Aury, I received from her hand-written cards and short letters. Our correspondence was polite and amicable but never intimate or deep in character. For the most part our letters concerned what we had been doing or reading. I sent her a copy of my first book when it appeared and she very kindly praised it. I sent her copies of a literary journal that I edited together with my wife. I always addressed her formally and respectfully by her full name.

Her early letters to me were without an opening salutation but by January of 1987 I was "Cher Gregory Stephenson" and she was signing herself "*tres affectuesement, votre vielle ami, Dominique.*" By September of that same year I had become "Cher ami," and a year later I was "Cher Gregory," remaining so thereafter. I cannot imagine that my letters to her could have meant much to her in her life, but she often thanked me for the fidelity and constancy of my attention to her, claiming repeatedly to have been touched by these qualities which she considered rare in the world.

In addition to this somewhat spare and sporadic correspondence with the author of *Story of O*, comprising sixteen letters altogether, on two occasions I also met and spoke with her. As in my correspondence, I avoided any suggestion that I believed her to be the author of *Story of O*. I felt that to make such an imputation (still less to confront her with a direct question on the matter) would be presumptuous and discourteous in the extreme.

The premise of my slender acquaintance with Dominique Aury was that of a shared interest in literature—though of course there was also in this an element of deception on my part. Despite my calculating camouflage, she would very likely have guessed that I thought her to be Pauline Réage, but I hoped that she appreciated my respectful reticence on the topic. On the other hand, it is possible that—once everyone was deceased who might be embarrassed by the revelation of her authorship of the scandalous *Story of O* – she was just waiting for someone to ask her, as did John de St. Jorre in 1994.[5]

I should also add that I was not attracted to the idea of *interviewing* Dominique Aury. I wanted to have a conversation with her. I took no notes during our talks but immediately afterward retired to my hotel room or to a quiet bar where I wrote down the substance and details of our talks.

My first meeting with Dominique Aury took place on the first of September in 1982, at the offices of Editions Gallimard and the *Nouvelle Revue Française* in Paris. We had agreed by telephone to meet at three in the afternoon. I brought with me gifts of a bottle of Danish mead and a bouquet of little pink flowers. We spoke in her narrow, neat office. Small in stature, she was dressed in a dark blue pants suit with a matching sweater worn over her shoulders. She wore a gold necklace and on her left hand a large gold ring (in the form of a scarab). Her gray-white hair was cut short and behind small reading glasses her eyes were a dark hazel color. She was very lightly made up, just the merest, most subtle touches to her cheeks and lips.

We talked at first of the *Nouvelle Revue Française,* its history and purpose. I then mentioned that I had once read a piece written by the German publisher, Max Niedermayer, concerning the life and thought of the dissident Freudian and pioneer of psychosomatic medicine, Georg Groddeck, in which she was mentioned as an ardent admirer of Groddeck's ideas. Yes, she replied, Groddeck's essential notion that there is an unconscious, unknown force within each of us that expresses itself through our lives – a hidden motive agency by which we are lived – was an idea that she found perspicacious. Her introduction to Groddeck's central work, *The Book of the It,* had come about when she had written a review for *Le Combat* of Lawrence Durrell's novel, *Justine.*

Durrell had very much liked her review and she had then been invited by him to a reception where he earnestly and eagerly commended Groddeck's work to her and loaned her a copy of *The Book of the It.* Upon reading it, she had found the book stimulating and insightful and had immediately thought that it *must* be published in French.

I asked Dominique Aury about her translations from English. These included, she said, two books by Arthur Koestler, *The Yogi and the Commissar* and *Promise and Fulfilment;* James Hogg's *Confessions of a Justified Sinner;* Thomas Browne's majestic *Urn Burial;* F. Scott Fitzgerald's *The Crack Up* and other short texts; *The Loved One* by Evelyn Waugh; and a personal favorite of hers, Stephen Crane's *The Red Badge of Courage.* She thought that John Houston's film of Crane's book was a rarity: a successful cinematic adaptation of a novel.

She had also translated Henry Miller's *Aller Retour New York* and in 1956 placed the book with a Swiss publisher in Lausanne. Without Dominique Aury's knowledge or consent, however, the publisher had removed from her translation all the obscenities and the lewd passages, publishing the book in that expurgated form. When Henry Miller discovered that his book had been bowdlerized he was very disappointed and when half-a-dozen years later he met Dominique Aury he reprimanded her for editing his book in this fashion. She explained to him what the Swiss publisher had done and proudly informed him that the book was soon to be printed by a French publisher for whom she was currently working to restore all the obscenities and the objectionable passages.

Among her most favorite translations from English was her version of Yukio Mishima's *Death in Midsummer* and a selection of his short fiction. There was a particular story by Mishima that she especially cherished, finding it altogether beautiful and believing also that the story represented the key to Mishima's life and work. The story was titled "Patriotism." She recounted to me the plot of this sad, lyrical, beautiful tale in which a Japanese officer and his wife commit hara-kari. Mishima himself, she told me, had expressed his pleasure in her translation (from English) preferring it to the other French translation (from the original Japanese) done by Gaston-Ernest Renondeau, a retired French general.

I inquired as to her family background and how it was that she came to study English. Her parents, she told me, were both of poor, peasant families. Her father was born in England because her grandparents had immigrated there during the Franco-Prussian war. Her grandfather had been a member of the *"francs tireurs,"* French partisans who fought against the invading Prussians and who were usually executed if captured.

Indeed, once her grandfather had been arrested by the Prussians on suspicion of being a partisan and had been led away with his hands bound before him, but he had managed to escape execution and had thereafter fled with his wife to England. There they remained for about twenty years, operating a small restaurant in Soho. In this way, her father was raised in England until he was nearly a young man. Her father was bilingual and had dual citizenship as well. She was raised reading English children's books, including Rudyard Kipling's *Just So Stories,* Lewis Carroll's *Alice in Wonderland,* and Thomas Hughes's *Tom Brown's School Days,* and others. An interest in English literature had seemed naturally to follow from these early experiences with English books.

Although she considered herself very much an anglophile, her deepest allegiances were to her home region of Brittany, to the landscape and the people. How she loved the austere Breton landscape, the rocky mountainous areas with sparse trees growing only where sheltered from the wind, the huge clouds scudding overhead, the wild ocean. She loved, too, the Breton people, their wildness, their pride, their affinity with the sea. The proudest claim in her family was to have had an ancestor who had served aboard a ship of the line against the English. There was, she said, an old saying that there were two kinds of Bretons, sailors and farmers, the former clean, the latter dirty.

She recounted how when she sailed to French Guinea in the company of Jean Paulhan, two of the five passengers on board the ship were Bretons. These two quickly announced to the other passengers that they were Bretons and whenever the ship docked at ports en route to Guinea it was the local Bretons who came to see what passengers were aboard, hoping that among them there might be fellow Bretons. She also related how once in a very small bar in a street off the rue Mouffetard she had seen two men performing a dance similar in movement to the Scottish Sword Dance, chanting as they danced: "Vive la Brétagne! Vive les Bretons!" The spectacle had stirred her deeply and had remained vivid in her memory. She very much admired this kind of attachment to a place and a people.

As to her family, the Desclos, they were Breton peasants, rooted in Brittany. It's only a peasant name, she said, but still ordinary people are often the best. There had been one black sheep in the Desclos family, one bad boy sometime in the 18th century who had gotten into some kind of scrape and had fled to the West Indies and was never heard of again. But after World War II when American troops had been billeted outside Paris, an American officer had contacted her father (who was then teaching English at a college near Paris) and told her father that he shared his surname and was a member of the New Orleans branch of the Desclos family descended from the young runaway and that the cemeteries of New Orleans were full of Desclos.

I asked her about her participation in the French Resistance movement during the war years. She shrugged modestly and said that her role had been very minor and unheroic. She had worked for *Lettres Françaises,* a clandestine journal. She was responsible for mailing and delivering copies of the journal, and sometimes books as well. In truth, she said smiling, she had been little more than an underground postmistress, and only very rarely had she been in any kind of danger.

There was about her person, I thought, a repose or poise, reflected in the quiet elegance of her appearance. At the same time, though, her eyes were alert, lively and humorous, and she spoke with animation, moving her body, her hands, making her face expressive. She was given to miming certain acts or events; for example, when she recounted the act of hara-kiri performed by the young officer in the Mishima tale, she formed both of her hands to mime the gripped knife and its motion. Or, later, when she told me how her grandfather was arrested and led away by the Prussians, she joined her wrists in such a way as to indicate that his hands were bound together and that he was pulled forward with a rope attached to them. And, again, when she related to me the Breton dance she had once witnessed in a bar, she mimicked for me the arm and body movements of the dancers. She was very courteous and gracious to me, signing my copy of *Literary Landscapes* with the inscription *"avec beaucoup de sympathie et très amicalement."*

My second meeting with Dominique Aury took place at the offices of Gallimard on the eleventh of April, 1989. She was now eighty-one years of age and looked thinner than when I saw her last. She was attired on this occasion in brown pants, a brown blouse and a brown sweater. Again, her only jewelry was a thin gold chain about her neck and the gold scarab ring on her hand. And, again, her make-up consisted of the merest, faintest tinting to her cheeks and lips. Her hair was now colored with a blue rinse. On her feet were laced brown half-boots.

I complimented her on the recent publication of a volume of Jean Paulhan's selected letters, *Choix de Lettres, 1917-1936,* of which she was co-editor.[6] The book had entailed enormous work, she said, but had been a labor of love and was a monument to a great intellect. A second volume was in preparation. I expressed my surprise at one incident referred to by

Jean Paulhan in a couple of his letters for the year 1927, that is a bitter quarrel that took place between Paulhan and André Breton, a quarrel so vehement that at length it led to Paulhan solemnly and in dead earnest challenging Breton to a duel. Yes, she smiled with a kind of wonder and admiration, Paulhan had actually engaged two of his friends to act as his seconds in the affair and had dispatched them to deliver his formal challenge to André Breton. Breton had quite simply refused to accept the challenge and Paulhan had thereafter viewed him as a contemptible coward.

The two men were not reconciled until twenty years had passed, she said. She was present on the night that their reconciliation took place, at a party given in honor of Breton's first publisher, at which both Paulhan and Breton were present. I sat to the right of Breton that night, she related. She thought Breton inflated with self-importance, much given to rhetorical flights and polemics. And his original insults to Paulhan had really been vicious, scurrilous and even threatening. Breton's enmity had been provoked by an article written in the *N.R.F.* by Paulhan under a pseudonym in which Paulhan had rather mildly criticized the surrealist group for their anti-literary stance. Paulhan's resort to duelling was not an isolated instance, she assured me, such challenges were not uncommon in France even in literary milieus. The practice of duelling did not altogether disappear until the German Occupation.

She also deplored the influence that Breton had exerted on so many writers and artists, an influence that she thought pernicious. Even André Pieyre de Mandiargues was awed by him, she told me, adding that she considered Mandiargues to be a far, far superior writer to Breton. This remark led us to discuss both Mandiargues's short fiction and his novels, *Le Lys de Mer, La Marge,* (for which he received the Prix Goncourt) and *La Motorcyclette,* which she admired. She had served on the committee for the Prix Fémina the year that *La Motorcyclette* appeared and wanted very much to award the prize to Mandiargues for that novel. She was rigorously opposed in this intention, though, by a very religious old lady on the committee who objected very strongly to the erotic content of Mandiargues's book. The lady "did not wish to have such a book on her conscience," as she herself expressed it. Dominique Aury was both annoyed and amused by this statement and told the lady that the erotic incidents described in the novel would scarcely be news to many people.

Somehow, we moved on to Proust and Céline, whom she considered to be the two great French writers of the 20th century and as utterly unlike each other as two writers might be. I mentioned that I had recently read a book concerning Céline's postwar incarceration in Denmark and how virulently he hated Denmark. Ah, he hated everything, she said, everything. So, Denmark was not special, she said smiling. She had met him after his release from prison and his return to France in the early 1950s and she found him insufferable as a man, but nevertheless a great stylist in French prose.

In contrast to the unrelenting catalog of the horrors and absurdities of war as described in certain of Céline's novels, she cited the far more inclusive and much more balanced perspective of Alfred de Vigny in his classic work, *Servitude et Grandeurs Militaires.* It could not be said that Vigny had neglected in his writing to depict the terrible events of war, the blunders and stupidities of the general staff, the appalling sufferings of the soldiers, but neither did he neglect to portray the beautiful acts of individual courage, the sublimity and nobility that are also aspects of war, though to say so has become unfashionable and unpopular, she added. She had long wished to write a full-length study of Vigny but unfortunately had never done so.

I mentioned that – inspired by her essay on Jacques Cazotte – I had read a Danish translation of *Le Diable Amoureux* and found it a singularly strange work, in some respects proto-surrealist in character. This semi-surreal element, she explained, derives in large part from the mystical or occult traditions in which Cazotte and several of his contemporaries were immersed. In Cazotte's writings hermetic allusions are made and these create startling, incongruous images. The occult traditions embraced by Cazotte are not French, she informed me, but Germanic, though through Cazotte and his direct heir, Gerard de Nerval, hermeticism entered French literature and the arts. I brought up Cazotte's prophecies concerning the advent and ultimate direction of the French revolution and his specific predictions concerning the coming fates of his acquaintances, predictions which proved to be true. Yes, she said, the incident was quite uncanny and inexplicable.

I said that I had read that in the 1930s an incendiary device was detonated at the offices of the *Nouvelle Revue Française.* Clearly, the magazine must have offended someone or some group more vindictive than André Breton and the surrealists. Was she working for the magazine at the time? Did she know who was responsible for the bomb or why it was directed at the *Nouvelle Revue Française*? She had not joined the *N.R.F.* until the 1940s, she said, and though she knew of the bomb she did not know who the perpetrators were or what ideology they had meant to further by their act. In those days, she said, everyone was so excitable, both on the right and the left. In those days, in 1934, she had attended a large political demonstration in which the police opened fire into the crowd.

She had thrown herself flat on the pavement, together with others around her. She had found the danger exhilarating and had subsequently attended demonstrations both of the right and the left merely for the excitement, the thrill of danger. Her husband had thought her mad for doing so. In fact, she was not in the least politically inclined and could not understand the fascination that politics has for so many people. In this regard, she mentioned *Bitter Lemons,* Lawrence Durrell's book on Cyprus, in which the first half of the book concerning the landscape and the people of the island is so charming and so absorbing, whereas the second half of the book, concerning the politics of the island, is so tedious as to be unreadable.

She had been fired upon again, on a later occasion, she told me. Once during the war she had been travelling with her young son, as part of a column of civilians, when an Italian pilot had repeatedly strafed the column. They had all taken cover in ditches alongside the road. She had shielded with her body her son who was crying in fear and she had calmed him by telling him that it didn't hurt to be killed by bullets, you didn't feel it. The column had quite unmistakably consisted of civilians, she said, yet the pilot dived and fired upon them again and again. I commented on the sheer malevolence of such an act. She shrugged and cited Lord Acton: "All power corrupts. Absolute power corrupts absolutely." The pilot was enjoying absolute power.

In this regard, she thought Conrad's *Heart of Darkness* an extremely prescient work. It could be read as a myth of the 20th century, she said, a metaphor not only for colonialism but for all the fanatical ideologies that had held sway in so many countries leading to mass murder and also for a darkness latent in the human heart.

The figure of Kurtz could be seen as a prophetic metaphor for the exercise of power that had led so many naïve idealists to perpetrate atrocities in the name of enlightened principles and also for certain other acts of mindless murder. Her father had told her of an incident in Chad where two French army officers "of the professional class" had gone amok, killing natives, shooting them, decapitating them, dismembering them. As in the case of Conrad's Kurtz or in the instance of the Italian pilot strafing the civilians, the potential for such purely malicious murderous behavior is always latent and may be suddenly called forth by a situation of supreme power. Truly, she said, Conrad had seen it clearly but no one had ever stated this psychological principle with greater vigor or conciseness of expression than Lord Acton.

It was because of this latent human capacity for senseless slaughter, she said, that she esteemed honest, honorable service in wartime. Her great-grandfather, her grandfather, and her father had served honorably in nearly all the wars of France. Her son had served in the Algerian war and had come home with his stomach ruined by disease. This ideal of honorable service was a quality she especially admired in the Bretons, together with their stubborn courage, their sense of personal dignity. They are often left in the lurch, she said, but they obey orders, they keep their word, they die to the last man. As they should, she added.

I noted again that Dominique Aury was alert and acute yet composed and self-possessed. In conversation she was very lively, speaking with her whole body, assuming postures and facial expressions, miming the actions that she was relating, indicating with her arms and her torso how she flung herself to the pavement when fired upon by the police and how she shielded her son beneath her when strafed by the Italian pilot. And yet even in relating these dramatic incidents it was as if she regarded them with a kind of detached fatalism.

It seemed to me that Dominique Aury (Anne Desclos) had worked out an independent and highly individual code by which she lived. The code derived from her awareness of dark ambiguities in the human psyche: destructive impulses, the urge for self-extinction, an aspiration to pure love, an appetite for the absolute. She was skeptical of all political programs to redeem or perfect humanity, persuaded that the roots of human suffering are to be found far beneath the social surface. Her private code was, I think, based on assent to fate rather than resistance to it. She believed that greater courage and resolve were required to embrace ones fate than to rebel against it. Although her literary tastes were clearly broad and inclusive, I think she valued most in literature that which illuminated the primal mysteries of love and courage, fidelity and death, themes as elemental and essential as the stark Breton landscape she loved.

In old French, the word "*desclos*" was the past participle of the verb *desclore,* meaning to open, unlock or reveal, and thus "*desclos*" meant open, exposed, plain, explicit. (The English word "disclose" derives from "*desclos.*") In one sense, the life of Anne Desclos, hidden as it was behind her pseudonyms, Dominique Aury and Pauline Réage, might seem anything but open, plain and exposed. In another sense, however, perhaps it was the pseudonyms themselves that served to quicken to life and give utterance to voices latent and hitherto silent in Anne Desclos. Perhaps, paradoxically, it was the masks, the disguises, the concealing names that permitted her to assert her true identity, to disclose secret selves.

Notes

1. *Story of O* by Pauline Réage, New York: Grove Press, 1965. Page references hereafter are to the paperback edition, Grove Press, 1967.

2. *Styles of Radical Will* by Susan Sontag, New York: Farrar, Straus & Giroux, p. 192.

3. *O m'as dit* by Régine Deforges, Paris: Jean-Jacques Pauvert, 1975.

4. *Lectures pour Tous* by Dominique Aury, Paris: Gallimard, 1958. The English translation is *Literary Landmarks,* London: Chatto & Windus, 1960. Page references hereafter are to this edition.

5. "The Unmasking of O" by John de St. Jorre, *The New Yorker,* August 1, 1994, pp. 42 – 50. Reprinted in *The Good Ship Venus, the Erotic Voyage of the Olympia Press* by John de St. Jorre, London: Hutchinson, 1994. A curious detail of John de St. Jorre's account of his interview with Dominique Aury whom he definitively identifies as Pauline Réage is his statement that these two names conceal "yet another persona, her true identity. She asked me not to reveal it, or the details of her family, and this I agreed to do" (231). I thought it had been for some long time and perhaps always common knowledge that Dominique Aury and Anne Desclos were one and the same. The *Dictionaire Biographique* that I consulted in 1980

stated quite openly that Dominique Aury was a pseudonym for Anne Desclos. And it will be recalled that I addressed my early letters to Anne Desclos at Gallimard, letters to which she replied signing herself by that name. Strange, then, that Dominique Aury extracted from John de St. Jorre a promise not to reveal what was already widely known and a matter of public record.

6. *Jean Paulhan, Choix de Lettres, 1917-1936,* edited by Dominique Aury and Jean-Claude Zylberstein, Paris: Gallimard, 1986.

Conversations with Berthe Cleyrergue, Housekeeper to the Legendary Amazon, Nathalie Clifford Barney

It was all still there. The small two-story house in the walled court-yard, the crumbling Grecian-style temple in a corner of the courtyard. On these premises many distinguished writers, artists and composers had stood chatting over cucumber sandwiches and cups of tea and many ar-dent lesbian love-affairs had been conducted. The street address was 20 rue Jacob, Paris, a dignified 17th century street in the 6th arrondisement. The now empty house in the courtyard was – for 60 years – the residence of Nathalie Clifford Barney, a wealthy American writer, affectionately called the Amazon (a name she proudly adopted) by her admirer Remy de Gourmont in tribute to her unabashed, openly acknowledged lesbianism. Born in Dayton, Ohio in 1876, Nathalie Clifford Barney lived nearly all of her life in Paris, dying there in 1972 at the age of ninety-five.

She is chiefly remembered (mentioned in two score of Paris memoirs and now the subject of half-a-dozen biographies) for her dauntless sexual escapades and for her role as hostess of a celebrated salon attended by such eminences as T.S. Eliot, Isadora Duncan, James Joyce, Gertrude Stein and Alice B. Toklas, Ezra Pound, Djuna Barnes, Edna St. Vincent Millay, William Carlos Williams and many others including prominent French scholars and authors. Nathalie Barney's salon was held on Fridays from 5 to 8 p.m., occasionally featuring literary readings, dance and mu-sical recitals. Fabled sandwiches and cakes were made and served by Miss Barney's long-time housekeeper, Berthe Cleyrergue. And even now in late December of 1981, the dilapidated old house, the deteriorating

Doric temple, the deserted cobblestone courtyard seemed to me still to hold something of the romance of the past.

I was very soon to discover – to my astonishment – that the house quite literally still held something of the romance of the past. As I strolled the grounds gazing at the old cobblestones, the withered garden, the walls and windows and doorways, my eyes fell upon the post box in the passageway. Written there in faded blue ink was the name "Cleyrergue." Was it possible, I wondered wildly, that Nathalie Barney's housekeeper still lived here? Charged with excitement and anticipation, I mounted the stairs to the first floor and rang the bell. The door was opened by a short, white-haired, bespectacled old lady. I recognized her at once from old photographs I'd seen. It was Berthe Cleyrergue.

I introduced myself, excusing myself for calling unannounced and explaining that I was interested in the life of Nathalie Clifford Barney. I had read, I told her, the biographies of Miss Barney written by Jean Chalon and George Wickes. (I said this intending to establish myself as having a serious interest in the subject.) My remarks, however, served to animate Berthe Cleyrergue. Jean Chalon, she told me vehemently, was guilty of many indiscretions, of distortions, errors and outright lies. And so, too, was George Wickes. She invited me into her dim low-ceilinged apartment and bade me sit down at a handsome old wooden table. She then seated herself next to me and showed me a book which she herself had written concerning her long acquaintance with Nathalie Clifford Barney (whom she called "Meez Bar-náy").

The book was titled *Berthe ou un demi siecle aupres de l'Amazone* (Berthe or half a century with the Amazon) and had only recently been published. She then commenced to guide me through the book photograph by photograph, discoursing at length on each in rapid Burgundian inflected French. It was clear that her memory was formidable. She named the month and year of each incident she recounted.

I was also impressed by Berthe's liveliness and apparent good health. She was 77 years old yet spry and supple, despite having undergone four operations necessitated, she told me, by having taken a fall in the cellar.

Berthe had entered into Miss Barney's service in June of 1927. The way in which this had taken place, she said, was through her previous acquaintance with Djuna Barnes who was a friend of Miss Barney. Berthe had formerly been employed in a shop in the 16th arrondisement where Djuna Barnes had been among her customers. Berthe had often made deliveries to the apartment where Djuna Barnes lived together with her lover, Thelma Wood. One day Djuna had confided to Berthe that she had carelessly caused a burn in the carpet of her rented apartment and that in compensation for this accident the landlord was demanding an enormous sum of money. Berthe had thought this unjust and had spoken with the landlord on Djuna's behalf.

The result had been that Djuna did not have to pay anything at all. After this incident the two women had become friends so that when Berthe had decided to seek some more interesting and remunerative employment, Djuna had encouraged her to apply to become a member of the household staff of Nathalie Clifford Barney and had recommended Berthe to Miss Barney. At the outset, Berthe told me, working at 20 rue Jacob as cook and maid, she was unaware of the nature of goings-on in the house.

When it first became clear to her that her employer was a notorious Lesbian, she thought she would quit (as so many before her had done.) However, since she was well-paid and well-treated and since the character of her work was often interesting, she decided, instead, to remain and soon grew to like and admire Miss Barney. Gradually, Berthe had taken on more and more responsibility for the managing of the house and had become not only housekeeper but a trusted confidante of her employer.

Not long after coming to work at 20 rue Jacob, Berthe had met Henri, the man who would become her husband. Henri, a man of various skills, had also proven to be very useful to Miss Barney who was well-pleased to have the pair living in the little apartment near the passageway. Henri had delighted in hunting and often contributed fresh game to the table of Miss Barney and her friends. Berthe had often supplied Gertrude Stein and Alice B. Toklas with partridges and pheasants shot by Henri, she said. Though these two ladies employed a servant, Toklas had reserved for herself the role of cook, even insisting on plucking the game birds herself. At the request of Toklas, Berthe added, she had later contributed a recipe for inclusion in Toklas' cookbook. (A casserole of mixed vegetables and veal.) Additionally, Berthe had often carried messages back and forth between Miss Barney and Gertrude Stein who lived nearby on the rue Christine. This was in the days before Miss Barney had a telephone installed.

The outbreak of the Second World War caught Miss Barney on a visit to Italy where she was obliged to remain for the duration of the conflict. During her absence Berthe dealt with all the many problems that arose concerning both the house and Miss Barney's personal possessions. (Nathalie Clifford Barney was considered Jewish by the Gestapo both because her sister was married to a member of the Dreyfus family and because her family background included a Jewish ancestor.)

Berthe was instrumental in saving Miss Barney's jewelry from confiscation and instrumental also in feeding Miss Barney's friends in Paris, many of whom were suffering under the chronic food shortages of the Occupation years. Berthe made numerous trips to the countryside returning with vegetables and fruit and even eggs and butter that she distributed free of charge to the friends of Miss Barney. After the war, when Miss Barney returned to Paris, as an expression of her gratitude she offered to Berthe several items from her personal jewelry including pearls, diamonds, bracelets and an expensive watch, but Berthe had refused to accept these gifts. Years later, however, she had been persuaded by Miss Barney to choose at the very least one item from among the jewelry bequeathed to Miss Barney by her dear friend, Liane de Pougny, and on this occasion Berthe had selected a small gold ring with a blue stone (the motif of the ring two nude women, bodies arched, hands reaching upward). Miss Barney had said to her: "Ah, Berthe, you have chosen well!"

Berthe's chief objection to the biographies of her former employer as written by Jean Chalon and George Wickes was that in her view these books concentrated overmuch on the intimate life of Nathalie Clifford Barney without understanding her personality as a whole. Of far greater importance to Miss Barney than her amorous attachments, Berthe said, had been her friendships. Friendship was sacred to her and she was very faithful and very generous to her many friends, both men and women. Berthe felt that after her many years of serving as guardian of the house and Miss Barney's affairs she now served as guardian of Miss Barney's reputation. That was why – as a corrective to what she saw as the more sensational and narrowly focused biographies written by Chalon and Wickes – she had recorded her own recollections of Miss Barney and her circle. The other biographies had also, Berthe observed, neglected to treat the seriousness of Miss Barney's authorship. Nathalie Clifford Barney had written plays, poems, a novel, memoirs, aphorisms. She had practiced a very strict work ethic with regard to her writing, Berthe said. It was a central and important aspect of her life. The biographers, she said, had scarcely mentioned this side of Miss Barney's personality.

A final more personal objection that Berthe expressed concerning both biographers was that they had in their books claimed ownership of the photographs she had lent to them and had failed to return to her not only photographs but also letters and others documents belonging to her that they had made use of.

Berthe said that she had been on excellent terms with nearly all of Miss Barney's regular visitors. She had read their novels and their poems (in French). This had been an education for her. She had conversed with them. They had signed her books. She cherished her memories of the distinguished writers she had met. The exception to her congenial relations to the many guests and friends was Miss Barney's last lover, Madame Lahovary. This affair had begun when Miss Barney was nearly 80 years of age and had lasted until her death. Berthe regarded Madame Lahovary as an intruder, an adventuress, a malign opportunist who had brought a destructive influence to bear upon Miss Barney's life, alienating her from her oldest and best friend, the artist Romaine Brooks. Berthe could not, she said, begin to understand the nature of Miss Barney's attraction to Madame Lahovary who was, in Berthe's opinion, so inelegant and uncultivated, altogether unlike the intelligent authors and artists with whom Miss Barney had associated all her life. But destructive attractions such as this are one of the greatest mysteries of life, Berthe said. They are incomprehensible. She had seen such relationships before, notably Djuna Barnes and her partner Thelma Wood.

At this point I was obliged to break off our conversation as I had to get back to my wife at our hotel. Berthe offered to meet with me again in just a few days. Eagerly and gratefully, I accepted an afternoon appointment with her early in the new year.

On the 2nd of January, 1982, at 4 p.m., about an hour before sunset, I opened the large wooden doors of 20 rue Jacob and entered the passageway. After admiring the carved griffins set in the wall of the passageway, I ascended the stairs and rang the bell of Berthe's apartment. She opened immediately and we greeted each other and wished each other a happy New Year. I presented her with a small pot of flowers that I had bought on the nearby rue de Buci. I could see that Berthe had dressed herself in more formal, more elegant clothes and was carefully coiffed and made up for our appointment. Again, we sat side by side at the fine old wooden table, this time going through an extraordinary album of photographs of Nathalie Clifford Barney.

The album included photographs of her as a child, a young lady, a woman, mature, older and then very old. There were photos of her father and mother, her sisters, her friends and lovers. These latter included Dolly Wilde, Djuna Barnes, Renée Vivien, Eva Palmer, the Duchess of Clermont-Tonnerre, Lucie Mardrus, Romaine Brooks, the author Colette, and Madame Lahovary (for whom Berthe again expressed disdain). Berthe's favourite among Miss Barney's friends was Colette, she said. They were both from Burgundy and this made for a special sympathy between them. And Berthe had very much enjoyed reading Colette's books.

Berthe commented on each photograph in the album, characterizing the person depicted or recounting an anecdote or incident she recalled. She pointed out to me similarities in the facial features of Miss Barney's ancestor (an officer in the American navy during the War of Independence) and those of Miss Barney. Berthe clearly preferred those photographs of Miss Barney where she looked most feminine and tended to disapprove of those in which she appeared in drag or a state of undress. Also contained in the photo album were a hand-written poem by Guillaume Apollinaire (a verse reply to an invitation-in-verse), and loosely inserted letters to Berthe from Djuna Barnes and from Dolly Wilde, as well as letters to Berthe from Nathalie Clifford Barney, from one of which Berthe read aloud to me a citation praising the commendable and indispensible service of Berthe and her husband, Henri.

Berthe asked me where I was staying in Paris and I replied that my wife and I were lodged in a hotel on the rue Git-le-Coeur. Oh, she said, Dolly Wilde had lived on that same street. (Dolly was the niece of Oscar Wilde and a flamboyant figure during the 1920s.) She had liked Dolly very much. Dolly was very lively and witty and they had laughed together many a time. Dolly Wilde was, Berthe said, "a marvellous being." They had been good friends, but Dolly had used drugs a great deal and was often in poor health. More than once, Berthe had nursed her carefully back to health. Miss Barney had also been extremely fond of Dolly, allowing her to stay in her house while she recuperated, giving her money, but because of Dolly's use of drugs the house had come under the scrutiny of the police. Berthe believed that it was Dr. Mahoney (Daniel Mahoney who served as inspiration for the immortal character of Dr. Matthew O'Connor in Djuna Barnes' novel *Nightwood)* who kept Dolly supplied with drugs. He lived nearby and was known to be an unsavoury type. Miss Barney would not allow him to enter her house.

Berthe said she had also nursed and cared for Djuna Barnes when after being abandoned by Thelma Wood she had succumbed to nervous exhaustion. Djuna had taken a room at the nearby Hotel d'Angleterre and Berthe had visited her there several times a day, bringing her food and little items of comfort, listening to her lamentations and attempting to assuage her despair. Djuna Barnes still wrote to her from New York, she said. Berthe showed me the most recent card she had received from her (strangely, it was written in English which Berthe can neither read nor speak.) I mentioned that I had a sporadic correspondence with Djuna Barnes and would be glad to convey Berthe's greetings to her and give her all of Berthe's news. Berthe expressed her pleasure at my offer, urging me to do so.

What impressions, I asked, did she have of Miss Barney? What opinion had she formed? Quite apart from Miss Barney's private life and her literary interests, what sort of person was she? She was, above all, Berthe said, very dignified, very proper, and very intelligent. She was, perhaps, somewhat reserved, not overtly affectionate or emotional, except once when she learned of the death of her dear friend, Romaine Brooks. Fundamentally, she was composed and collected but she could suddenly fly to pieces in the face of some minor problem. She was also quite particular about things; she had firm ideas of how certain things – furniture, objects, routines – should be in her household and insisted that they must be that way. Yet other things – like the condition of the house itself – she ignored and neglected. She was obstinate in many ways, Berthe thought, strong-willed. But also generous and understanding. She enjoyed companionship and good food.

In the company of her American friends, Miss Barney was much given to laughter, Berthe said. Sometimes they laughed and laughed. As she did not herself understand English, Berthe had no idea what the topics of these hilarious conversations might have been. Miss Barney had not interfered in matters of housekeeping. She had never been meddlesome but had given Berthe free rein in all things, trusting her completely with household expenses and accounts. Miss Barney had also frequently consulted Berthe on questions of apparel and appearance, soliciting her reactions and preferences in regard to clothing and jewelry. Miss Barney had even asked her opinion of certain guests but in such matters Berthe had declined to offer her estimations, thinking it better to keep her own counsel.

In providing dinners and refreshments for Miss Barney's salon and her gatherings, Berthe said she had learned many things and had enjoyed her work preparing food, despite its demanding nature. She had learned to make a large variety of sandwiches and she had even learned to cook Thanksgiving dinner according to the American tradition. Miss Barney observed this feast every year with her American friends. All these things had been relatively easy before the war but after the war there was scarcity and rationing. Then, it had been difficult to obtain the right materials and ingredients.

Berthe served me a drink that she described as a Burgundian specialty: a mixture of sirop de cassis and white wine. And she plied me with delicious small cookies and candies arranged on a small silver platter.

This is as close, I thought, as I will ever come to attending one of the fabled Fridays at 20 rue Jacob. And how exhilarating for me it is to have this encounter with a living witness to a mythic era, someone who sees in the eye of memory Sylvia Beach, Gertrude Stein and other figures of that remote, romantic time. Berthe's small apartment was crowded with furnishings she had managed to salvage from Nathalie Clifford Barney's house including the table at which we sat and the chairs on which we're sitting. Most of Miss Barney's furnishings had been sold at auction, she told me, often for a pittance. Berthe also possessed many paintings and drawings by Romaine Brooks and other artists, together with many books signed and dedicated to her by the various authors who frequented the salon over the years. It was evident that she took considerable pride in showing me these things. She had made provisions, she said, that upon her death her photographs, books and letters were to be donated to the Jacques Doucet library which already housed a collection of books and letters by Nathalie Clifford Barney.

Perhaps it was the word *death* that caused me suddenly to think of the sheer strangeness of our meeting, two humans from opposite ends of the earth together in a room in Paris on a winter evening, speaking of the past, of the dead. And soon, thanking Berthe profusely and promising to write, I put on my coat and took my leave. Walking away from 20 rue Jacob in the darkness, I recalled a line from a poem by Ezra Pound (with whom Nathalie Clifford Barney often played tennis): *"She was a very old lady, I never saw her again."* And, indeed, that was how it was to be.

Tête-à-Tête with the Frog Prince: Conversations with Maurice Girodias

Rogue publisher and himself a bit of a rogue, Maurice Girodias, founding editor of the infamous Olympia Press, chief purveyor of English language pornography during the postwar period, loosed upon an eager reading world a handful of scandalous masterpieces together with what were (by his own bemused admission) torrents of bad taste. The publication of modern classics such as Samuel Beckett's *Watt,* Vladimir Nabokov's *Lolita,* J.P. Donleavy's *The Ginger Man,* William S. Burroughs' *The Naked Lunch,* as well as notable works by Jean Genet, Henry Miller, Lawrence Durrell and Jean Cocteau was made possible by the sale of a series of pseudonymously written sexually explicit novels with lubricious titles such as *Chariot of Flesh, White Thighs, Sin for Breakfast* and *There's a Whip in my Valise.* Published in Paris, Olympia books were forbidden throughout the English-speaking world but were smuggled through Customs by returning tourists, merchant seamen, servicemen and others.

The mixture of literature and lust reflected in the publications of Girodias' Olympia Press may perhaps be seen as an expression of divisions within the man himself whose behaviour encompassed shady practices and impetuous generosity, irrepressible audacity and shy reserve, conspicuous dissipation and secret spirituality. Indeed, I have sometimes speculated whether his often turbulent personal fortunes were not, at least in part, the result of a species of subconscious self-sabotage.

A self-described "second-generation pornographer," Maurice Girodias was born Maurice Kahane in Paris in 1919, the son of English expatriate author and publisher, Jack Kahane, proprietor of the Obelisk Press. Racy, risqué novels in English were the speciality of the Paris-based Obelisk Press and Kahane's prize literary discovery was Henry Miller.

Upon the sudden death of Jack Kahane at the outbreak of World War II, young Maurice inherited the debt-ridden Obelisk Press, but the war and the German occupation (during which to avoid deportation as a Jew, Maurice changed his surname to that of his French mother) compelled him instead to establish himself as an art publisher, forming his own imprint, Les Editions du Chêne. After the war, the presence in Paris of large numbers British, Canadian and American soldiers (and later, the return of tourists) provided Maurice with a readership sufficient to resurrect the Obelisk Press and reissue the more popular titles of its prewar catalog.

According to Girodias' version of events, it was due to the machinations of his business partners, Hachette Publishers, that he lost ownership of both Les Editions du Chêne and the Obelisk Press. After an extended period of poverty and depression, in the early 1950s Girodias succeeded in founding the Olympia Press on little more than daring and desperate desire. Slowly, Olympia attained a precarious solvency, then – largely as a consequence of the popularity of *Lolita* and a favourable contract with Vladimir Nabokov – achieved outright prosperity.

This pleasantly unwonted circumstance proved, however, less than a boon for Girodias for it permitted him to indulge in an extravagant, not to say grandiose, project: the creation of a lavish, sumptuous nightclub called La Grande Séverine, an unrealistically ambitious undertaking that was an economic disaster.

Closely related – both in terms of cause and effect – to this reckless enterprise was Girodias' excessive drinking. At the same time, the Olympia Press was being relentlessly harassed by the Paris vice squad and was the object of manifold lawsuits. At length, his personal life out of control, his nightclub bankrupt, his press paralyzed by punitive fines and publishing bans pronounced by the courts, Girodias fled to the United States to re-establish the Olympia Press in New York City.

Arriving in America in the mid 1960s, Girodias busily set about making and losing fortunes. Recently liberalized federal laws concerning the censorship of printed matter and a changing cultural climate in the U.S. helped to ease his path as a publisher of pornography while at the same time serving to stimulate the development of competing publishers in the same field, some of whom shamelessly pirated Girodias' Paris publications (few of which had been copyrighted.)

Ever inventive, ever enterprising, by sheer will and ingenuity, for over a decade Girodias kept his American venture in operation, enjoying intermittent prosperity and enduring recurrent fiasco. Forced at last by adverse circumstances to abandon the Olympia Press, he formed the Freeway Press (later Venus-Freeway Press). At length, however, in a final debacle all schemes and hopes collapsed. Thereafter, for a time, Girodias lived a quiet life in Boston with his latest wife, writing his memoirs. Then, when his marriage failed, weary and indigent he returned to Paris.

The first volume of Girodias' autobiography, covering the years from his childhood to the Second World War, was published in France in 1977 under the title *J'arrive*. In 1980 the book appeared in English as *The Frog Prince*. In neither language, though, did the book attract more than scant notice. Nor were the meagre royalties that Girodias received for the indifferent sales of the book sufficient to alleviate his now chronic penury. He was reduced at last to living with family members and friends, with frequent changes of address.

In the spring of 1982, I initiated a correspondence with Maurice Girodias, one that was to continue intermittently until only a few months before his sudden and untimely death in early July of 1990. During this same time, on two occasions, I met and spoke with Maurice in Paris. Our first meeting took place in September of 1982. I was accompanied by my

wife, Birgit. At the time Girodias was living at number 20 Quai de Bé-
thune on the Ile St. Louis, a solid 17th century sandstone building with
white shutters and black wrought iron balconies. His name did not appear
among the occupants of the building at the main entrance so I pressed the
button designated as "Gardien," and inquired of the concierge if Mon-
sieur Girodias lived there. She informed us that he lived on the 4th floor
and buzzed us into the building. We passed through the heavy studded
wooden doors (with sculpted demonic faces on either side of the doorway
and a winged angel in relief across the frieze) ascended flights of stone
steps and walked wooden landings. Above the apartment doors were bas
reliefs with classical motifs. Reaching the fourth floor (or fifth floor as
counted by Americans) we rang the doorbell. A woman answered and we
explained the purpose of our visit. She invited us in and went to fetch
Girodias who then showed us into the kitchen where we sat and spoke.
There appeared to be five other occupants of the apartment.

Our conversation begins in French then drifts into English. Girodias
is equally at ease in either language but speaks English with a slight
French accent. The apartment is not his, he explains; he is merely staying
there with friends. When did he return to Paris, I ask. He thinks it was in
October of the preceding year. Girodias is a handsome man with silver-
gray hair combed straight back, a sort of hawk nose, white, even teeth and
sad dark-brown eyes. He wears a brown shirt unbuttoned at the neck ex-
posing a gray-haired tanned chest. He has the air of one who has just
awakened from sleep and has not yet altogether collected his thoughts.
He seems somewhat abstracted, absent. He offers us a glass of red wine
which we accept and we sit drinking at the kitchen table. Have you any
projects at present, I ask. He replies that he is working on plans for a new
magazine he wants to publish and edit. The magazine is to be called
America, and it will concern itself with American fashion and film, American literature and culture, American food and trends and American

thought. The French, he says, in common with nearly everyone everywhere, have a love-hate relationship with the United States. This magazine will address their half-sceptical, half-fascinated interest in things American. He needs about one and a half million dollars to launch it. His weary smile indicates that he thinks it highly unlikely that he will ever find investors to provide the necessary capital.

What is his legal status in France at present, I ask. Has the ban on publishing imposed on him back in the 1960s been lifted? It's still uncertain, he says. He has applied to the authorities for formal "rehabilitation," they have promised to address the question, but it's quite a complicated matter. He shrugs. He can in any case work through friends, using their names. But a judicial declaration of "rehabilitation" would be good publicity for him. It would bring him some favourable attention and it might help attract investors, he says. I ask him about his memoirs. When might the second volume appear? He  has written some of it, he says, but he was discouraged by the poor sales of the first volume and has laid the manuscript aside.

Fundamentally, he questions the value of the subject matter. He does not feel that he can claim any insights regarding Beckett, Nabokov or Burroughs. Perhaps, too, in order to avoid controversy and possible litigation it would be better to wait until those he intends to discuss in his memoirs are already dead. And in any case, he finds writing to be very demanding and troublesome and thinks his own writing of dubious worth.

The writing of the first volume was a curious process, he says. At first he just sharpened his pencils and stared at the blank paper before him. He could not seem to get started. Whole mornings and afternoons passed in this manner. At last, however, he began to write and once begun he wrote day and night for three and a half weeks. To sustain his powers of recollection, he had continually smoked good quality marijuana while outside it was a snowy New England winter encouraging a certain inwardness and reflection. As he wrote he began to remember incidents and people he had not recalled or thought about for a great many years. The account of his life that he had set down was about 99 per cent true, he says, there was only a little invention involved on his part. Indeed, there were certain incidents which he had felt compelled to tone down in order to make them seem more credible. The finished manuscript had numbered about 700 pages which the publisher had edited down to about 500 pages.

We talk then of his ill-fated Danish publishing venture in the mid 1960s which had consisted both of a Danish language version of the Olympia Press and another imprint called The Odyssey Library which was an English language press designed to circumvent the publishing ban placed upon Girodias by the French courts. Girodias had aimed to print and distribute a new line of erotic novels from Copenhagen. Some half-a-dozen titles had been printed.

Curiously, though, the French police had somehow persuaded the Danish police to confiscate the publications of the Odyssey Library and this despite the fact that the books were in English and despite liberal Danish laws then in force that protected the written word, including pornographic literature. To have been banned in Denmark! He smiles ruefully and shakes his head in amused disbelief. His partner in Denmark had been honest in all his dealings with him, Girodias says, and that was rare, indeed, among persons of that milieu. Unfortunately, however, his Danish partner had died suddenly. The man's son had then taken over and if equally honest was less competent than his father. "A second generation pornographer – just like me," Girodias says. Another factor that had contributed to the misfortunes and ultimate collapse of Girodias' Danish venture had been the advent of the legalization – first in Denmark then elsewhere – of visual pornography. Erotic novels had been a casualty of the unfolding sexual revolution.

I mention the persistent misapprehension that those Olympia titles written under the pseudonym of Akbar del Piombo were authored by William S. Burroughs. I firmly believe this attribution to be incorrect, I say, but does he know the origins of the myth? Girodias says that he once ascertained the cause of this mix-up – an error which has since been a source of irritation to both authors – but he has now forgotten what it was. (He could now remember much less concerning the events of recent years, he says, than those of the more distant past.)

He believes that it was a mis-print in an announcement or catalog that gave rise to the confusion. It was certainly not deliberate on his part, he says, as some have implied – a ruse to increase sales of the Akbar del Piombo books. He would not have done such a thing, nor would the two authors have countenanced it. (Years after this conversation, I believe I discovered the source of the error. The second printing of the one-volume trilogy of novels by Akbar del Piombo collectively titled *The Fetish Crowd* was in June 1965 at the Imprimerie Croutzet in Paris. At the same time, June 1965, a second printing of William S. Burroughs *The Naked Lunch* was undertaken for Olympia by the same local printer. Inadvertently, a page from the front matter of the latter book was bound into the former, a page listing "Other works by William Burroughs published by the Olympia Press" including *The Soft Machine* and *The Ticket that Exploded.* Many readers – and some libraries – took this to mean that Akbar del Piombo and William Burroughs were one and the same.) Norman Rubingon was, of course, the author behind the Akbar del Piombo pseudonym. He had seen Rubington only last year in New York City, he says. He was living near the Bowery, surviving, "a lazy bum," Girodias pronounces affectionately.

Girodias says that he is often astonished and disappointed to learn that certain of his best authors from the old Olympia days, those he thought most promising, had, in fact, done their best work writing for him. Alexander Trocchi, for example, who was clearly the most talented of the young postwar expatriate writers had produced very little of significance after 1960. Trocchi had, of course, been terribly addicted for many years now and had been very ill.

Trocchi is now, he believes, a bookseller in London. The subsequent writing career of Iris Owens, in particular, had been a great disappointment and surprise to him. He had thought her very talented and destined to become an important writer but she had seemed to lose inspiration with the loss of the Olympia DB (dirty book) structure and the freedom to experiment that comes with writing under a pseudonym.

The expatriates of the postwar period, he says, were in the main rather insular, frequenting only two cafés, not learning to speak French (some of them even after 10 years in Paris) or having any contact with the French. Then during the Algerian war some expatriates had been harassed or expelled by the police under the tightening of regulations that were instituted then. It was then, Girodias says, that they discovered that "France is a Fascist country -- as every Frenchman already knows."

I ask if any of the correspondence, the manuscripts and other documents of the Olympia Press remain. No, he says, everything was thrown away by the landlord of the building in 1968, while he himself was in New York. Except for some Henry Miller letters which the landlord sold to a collector. The only part of those archives whose loss is truly regrettable, Girodias says, was a file containing some of the insane letters received over the years by the Olympia Press. He smiles to remember them.

There were the most extraordinary letters from, among others, credulous customers, lechers of all nations, lunatic lonely hearts and furious Head Masters of English public schools. Girodias had made a selection of the best of them – the most entertaining, the most poignant – which he'd kept in a file, intending to publish the collection as a book.

Those letters, he says, were indeed a unique treasure and were truly irreplaceable. In fact, he adds, he has no material at all pertaining to his career as a publisher and he doesn't even own a copy of a single one of all the many books he published, though he thinks that his brother Eric might have some few of them.

Girodias is amazed and amused at my interest in his past publishing activities. When I mention certain titles – such as *Boy* and *To Beg I am Ashamed* – that he reprinted under the Obelisk imprint in the immediate postwar years, he expresses surprise that he did so. "Gee, did we really do those?" he asks. He never suspected, he says, that one day collectors and university librarians would seek out all those drab little volumes. They were, after all, so undistinguished in appearance. The quality of the paper and the printing was poor. He had chosen the format for the pocket-sized Traveller's Companion Series precisely because books of those dimensions were more suited to smuggling in pockets. His earlier books had been too large and bulky. The drab green color of the books had also been chosen for its property as camouflage; the color was "the very opposite of flashy." This, too, had been to facilitate smuggling the books past Customs Inspectors who nevertheless had had an uncanny ability to "nose them out."

On one occasion, he had himself been stopped upon entering England with a selection of Henry Miller's works in his suitcase. "Naughty, naughty," the Customs Inspector had said to him, "those are forbidden here." Girodias says that he explained to the Customs man that as a Frenchman he hadn't known they were forbidden and that at the request of an English friend he was only bringing them to the man as gifts. The Customs Inspector had then allowed him to pass with the books, thinking him to be an elderly, naïve Frenchman, little suspecting that he was the very man responsible for publishing the books in question.

He regrets, he says, neglecting the Olympia Press and draining away its financial resources on his ill-fated nightclub during the late 1950s and early 1960s. He can now remember but little of that period, he admits, as he'd spent those years drinking to excess and keeping late hours in his nightclub. But he can clearly see that his heedless behavior contributed to the downfall of the Olympia Press. However, it must be said, he adds, that others also did their part in undermining his enterprise. Austryn Wainhouse and Dick Seaver at Grove Press took over much of the list he had built up, including Beckett and Genet, Pauline Réage, Henry Miller and Burroughs. In addition, in imitating Olympia's practice of bringing back into print classic erotic works, Grove had taken from him a vital part of his very *raison d'etre* as a publisher. Worse, though, pirate publishers – such as Brandon House, Greenleaf and Collector's Publications – had re-printed almost all of his Paris books without his permission or that of the authors and had paid neither fees nor royalties.

These were the very books and authors that Girodias had so carefully nurtured in Paris, books for which he had paid authors the standard fee and for which he had endured police harassment, arrests and court battles, fines and prohibitions, books which had cost him bribe money and lawyers' fees. His Olympia books had also been pirated in the Far East, in Taiwan, in India, appearing in smudgy editions printed on disintegrating paper, novels recombined, titles switched. The pirates had plundered his livelihood, he says. Not only were their practices reprehensible but they showed a deplorable lack of originality.

Yet in recounting this litany of misfortunes Girodias betrays little bitterness. He seems instead mildly amused by the various turns of fortune he has experienced. (I think of the Chinese writer, Lu Hsun, who observed: "I believe that those who sink from prosperity to poverty probably come, in the process, to understand what the world is like.") He consents courteously to Birgit's request to take a photograph of him, though modestly remarking that he considers himself highly unphotogenic. He signs our copy of *The Frog Prince* with a friendly and generous inscription. My impression is of a very likeable, affable man, sad, defeated but sustained by a wry and weary humour.

During the years that followed, Girodias and I kept up our intermittent correspondence. I noted the frequent changes of address on his letters. He kept me abreast of his (ultimately futile) attempt to reach a pecuniary settlement with Collins/Grafton publishers for their having pirated certain of his original Olympia books. He had by now, he confessed, lost his taste for litigation. Nor could he any longer afford legal counsel. Sheer economic necessity obliged him to continue scuffling and scraping to make a living. Since he had no archives whatever with regard to his past publishing activities, I willingly furnished him with copies of articles from my own extensive files concerning the Olympia Press. These were pieces which had appeared in *Time, Evergreen Review, The Spectator, Publishers Weekly* and elsewhere. These were, he wrote me, very helpful to him in writing his memoirs.

My second conversation with Maurice Girodias took place in April of 1989. At Girodias' suggestion, we made a rendezvous at Le Bonaparte, a café on Place Saint-Germain-des-Prés. I arrived a bit early and secured one of the small tables along the rear wall of the café from which I would be able to see people entering. I ordered a glass of Campari and waited. Girodias arrived a bit late, wearing dark slacks and a dark sport coat, a white shirt open at the neck. I thought he looked more brisk and buoyant than on our previous meeting seven years previous. He still retained that look of amused and ironic detachment which comes to men who have experienced dramatic reversals and inversions of fate. He apologized for being late, then asked me what my drink was and ordered the same from the waiter. We talked amid the clinking and clattering of cups and glasses and the chatter of the other café guests.

My opening question to him, again, concerns his current projects. He is editing an issue of *The Courier,* a magazine put out by UNESCO, he tells me. The theme of the issue is that of beauty in all its expressions. It's progressing satisfactorily, though he expects to deliver the material about a month past the deadline he has been given. But they expect that, he adds. The topic of beauty is one that interests and engages him deeply, he says. In the wake of the sexual revolution, the time is now propitious for "the beauty revolution," which will mean an exploration and appreciation and deeper understanding of all aspects of beauty.

The beauty revolution will be a kind of metaphysical counterpart to the sexual revolution, both its antithesis and its complement, its fulfilment. He would like to edit a book, a collection of essays, on the same theme. In this regard, he would wish to gather essays on various aspects of beauty from experts in particular fields. For example, he would like to have an essay on the beauty of light written by an astrophysicist. The difficulty, he says, is in getting highly informed views on such a subject that are at the same time exciting to read. He would like contributions that are elegant and innovative as well as authoritative.

He is also currently attempting to start a new publishing venture, a series of books that would be projections, predictions of "the utopias of the third millennium." Again, these would be written by various hands whose expertise is in the area of art, society, and a range of other pertinent subjects. He has, he says, already found a banker who will invest 60 per cent of the required capital. He, himself, must now raise the remaining 40 per cent. He probably can't do so, he says smiling, but who knows?

What is the status of the second volume of your memoirs, I ask. He has given it up again, he says. At least temporarily. He has now written about two-thirds of the second volume but thinks that what he has written lacks form, as well as lacking an informing perspective both on the events and on himself. And without such a perspective the tale of his life lacks coherence. Essentially, he questions "the value of such paltry personal reminiscences" in the context of truly significant world events. And quite apart from such reservations, it bores him to go over again that period of his life. Nor can he imagine that many readers would be interested in his account. Finally, the narrative is not a success story and so it has neither appeal nor any point as such. I object that it is really rather an extraordinary story, certainly one that has interested me intensely. He thanks me for my kindness and concedes that there are a few droll episodes. There is, for example, the sorry tale of his 21 year feud in the courts with J.P. Donleavy. Although it was Donleavy who ultimately triumphed, Girodias finds the denouement – in which he was craftily out-maneuvered by his relentless adversary – to be no less amusing for his own discomfiture.

At issue between publisher and author was a question of breach of contract on the part of Donleavy. After many years and much litigation and lawyers' fees in plenty, Girodias had still believed he could win the case. In the French courts, he had already won some preliminary judgements against Donleavy. He was, however, yet once again, bankrupt. The Paris Olympia Press as an entity was also broke, in debt, and was to be sold for payment to creditors.

If Girodias could regain ownership of the Olympia Press he could press on with his suit against Donleavy. Accordingly, when the Olympia Press was to be set at auction, Girodias contrived (by means of bribes) to have the auction take place as quietly, even secretly, as possible. He even succeeded in having the legally required newspaper announcements of the auction quashed. In this way, he hoped to buy back his press as cheaply as possible and with it the Donleavy contract. He was dismayed, then, on the afternoon of the auction to see others present in the secluded room where the auction was to take place. Present were two women and their lawyer. One of the women glared at him with undisguised hostility. This was ominous, unsettling. He had no notion of who they might be or how they had learned of the auction.

As the bidding began, Girodias was constantly, casually outbid by the lawyer for the two women. Their final bid exceeded all the capital he could possibly hope to borrow. He had definitively lost the Olympia Press and the two women were now the owners of his life's project and all its prospects. Even in his black dejection, Girodias wondered who they were and why they had visited upon him such destruction. Not long afterward, compounding his loss, he discovered that one of the women was Donleavy's wife. Donleavy, his long-time legal adversary and arch-foe, now owned the Olympia Press.

Donleavy, Girodias remarks, was, indeed, the Ginger Man, but without the charm. He was a ruthless, vindictive man, a monstrous egotist. Moreover, all Donleavy's novels since *The Ginger Man* were inferior and repetitive. He had never developed as a novelist. He had but the one trick, the one formula that had made his name. Through the intermediary of a New York reporter, Girodias had recently proposed to Donleavy that they collaborate on a book in which each party would relate his side of the story. Donleavy had ignored the offer. I don't understand his unending animosity, Girodias says, after all it is he who has won. Indeed, Girodias adds, Donleavy won doubly, as it were.

The Olympia Press was a salutary event, I tell him. It was entirely *sui generis,* a kind of Wild West of literature. The pizzazz, the panache, the mad humour, the exuberance. The preposterous noms-de-plumes, the extravagant sexual antics recounted in the "dirty books." Norman Rubington's crazy collage novels. Yes, he agrees, the humour had not been fully appreciated. Even Rubington had at first been unpleasantly surprised by the wildly incongruous pseudonym that Girodias had chosen for him (i.e. Akbar del Piombo). Rubington had objected, saying "I'm a New York Jew and you've given me an Arab name!" At the outset of the whole nefarious Olympia enterprise, Girodias says, he was very fortunate in having Trocchi as a literary collaborator. Trocchi had a genius for that sort of thing. Girodias had suggested to him that he write a kind of contemporary *Fanny Hill,* using that novel with its female narrator and the record of her erotic misadventures as a model, and Trocchi had done so brilliantly in *The Carnal Days of Helen Seferis.* Thereafter, Girodias says, he had given that novel by Trocchi to his other prospective Olympia Press writers to use as a template for their efforts.

Trocchi had been the central figure of the postwar expatriate group, Girodias says, the dominant personality, the one whose tastes and inclinations influenced many of the others. But he had been a strange man who had "tried to cheat his way through life." Unfortunately, Trocchi had dissipated his very considerable gifts in writing pornography for the Olympia Press. It seems to have undermined his faith in the value of writing, Girodias says. Another promising writer whose pornographic novels for Olympia had been better than her subsequent literary efforts was Iris Owens, he says. Perhaps it was as Oscar Wilde had written somewhere about the truth of masks. ("Man is least himself when he talks in his own person. Give him a mask and he will tell you the truth.")

It was, he says, as if the pseudonyms assigned these authors had released them from an oppressive self-consciousness and from preconceptions about literature and conventions of what constitutes good writing. Liberated by their disguises, they had enjoyed creative freedom, exercising considerable inventiveness and imagination in their writing, even engaging in radical experimentation, as in Harriett Daimler's (Iris Owens) *The Organization.* Iris Owens, he says, had later attempted to imitate her own DBs for the mainstream literary market, but had done so with indifferent results.

He has not recently seen Iris Owens, he says, nor do they correspond. But when last he saw her in New York City she was as witty and as pretty as ever. Mason Hoffenberg is dead as of 3 years ago. Rubington came to Paris on a visit a few years ago but seemed a bit distant. Trocchi is dead. It's all a long time ago now. The principals are all scattered and one by one they are disappearing. It was great fun, he says, but in the end it was of little consequence.

I, of course, politely object to this estimate of the Olympia Press and ultimately Girodias accedes to my assertion that the Olympia enterprise was a vital aspect of the postwar cultural revolution, that it not only prefigured but precipitated certain elements of the rebellious 1960s. My own view, I tell him, is that the much celebrated 1960s were, in fact, a kind of parody of the 1950s, a weak imitation of the experimental aesthetics and the more unconventional currents of thought of that earlier era. Yes, Girodias agrees, but the Fifties were in their turn a kind of parody of the 1930s. The literary expatriates in Paris in the Fifties had been attempting to repeat the experiences of the earlier wave of expatriate writers. They had seen themselves as contemporary heirs to Hemingway or Henry Miller but they had lacked both the talent and the originality of those authors. George Plimpton, in particular, had struck him as a kind of counterfeit litterateur. Plimpton had, in fact, once written a DB for Olympia that he had turned down. It made unpleasant reading and was distinctly inferior in quality, Girodias says.

His own biggest mistake, Girodias says, was the nightclub, La Grande Séverine. He should never have entered into such an endeavour. He knew nothing about the practicalities of such a business, he says, and it had ended in a financial debacle. Since then, of course, he had experienced bankruptcies so numerous that he couldn't keep track of them, financial reverses and the failures of myriad enterprises had since been so frequent, one following hard on the heels of another. He had prospered in New York, he said, largely due to an excellent business partner, an ex-sailor, "a businessman-thief." This man, he says, had had excellent qualifications and connections for that shady line of publishing and for a time he had made Girodias a millionaire. And this had been accomplished in spite of the legalization of pornography in the U.S. and despite all the piracies of the original Olympia novels, many of which were simply photo-offset from Girodias' Paris publications, and despite a horde of competitors in the field. But with his newly won prosperity, Girodias had overreached. He had, he says, tried to build a publishing empire on a world scale, with ventures in Holland, Italy, Germany, Japan, and elsewhere. He had even had a scheme that involved translating pornographic novels into Russian.

These books were to be sold in Finland to Russian sailors who would then smuggle them back into their country as in the old, original Olympia days. Sailors had always been some of his best customers, he says. In the 1950s when the U.S. fleet would anchor in the south of France, he would dispatch enormous shipments of Olympia books there as quickly as he could to meet their reading needs. He had often reflected that bell-bottomed trousers such as sailors wear are ideal for smuggling books.

But now it is all gone, all over, he says. Fortunes had been won, lost, won again, then lost again. "Now I *have* to change my luck," he says. "I have nothing. I must strive and provide for myself however I can." Accordingly, he still pins desperate hopes on his current projects while at the same time doubting the likelihood of their realization. Sometimes in the past he had prospered by bluff and sheer luck, but perhaps those days are now definitively over. I ask if the court ban imposed on his publishing is still in force. He thinks not, though he would be banned anyway for having filed bankruptcy so many times. Had he ever inquired under the Freedom of Information Act as to whether there was an FBI file on him, I ask, had he ever attempted to get ahold of it? No, he replies, he believes that in order to petition for information of that nature you have to sign an affidavit at the U.S. Embassy and he is reluctant to draw undue attention to himself from that quarter. He wants to maintain his ability to re-enter the United States. He adds that his FBI file probably "goes back to before my birth."

I ask Girodias if I may pose a rather personal question, concerning his spiritual beliefs. He widens his eyes and wiggles his ears in mock horror, then smiles and nods. I mention that in his autobiography, *The Frog Prince,* he recounts how as a youth and during his young manhood he embraced Theosophy, attended lectures by Krishnamurti, pursued an earnest interest in Eastern thought. Does he still hold such beliefs? Girodias replies that he does. Even as a drunkard, even as the King of Porn, he says, he retained his original perspective on the self and the spirit. He had often felt, he says, as if all the dissipation, the sensual self-indulgence, the rapid changes of fortune he had known in his life were somehow something he had to endure, almost an ordeal. Something to do in some way with expiation or purgation or satiety. Inwardly, he has, he says, remained true to his youthful self and to the spiritual path he chose in those early years. Indeed, he feels as if he is the same person merely inhabiting an older body, "surprised to be an old man."

With regard to the spiritual beliefs he embraced early in his life, concerning karma, death and the survival of consciousness, he says that he continues to hold the same beliefs and he has always felt that life would be utterly absurd without the survival of the spirit. He has never questioned that it endures and evolves. Whatever his personal failings had been and despite the many changes of outward circumstance that he had experienced, a belief in the journey of the spirit had remained fundamental to his understanding of existence.

I mention that for me the most haunting passages of his autobiography were those recounting the strange experiences he underwent night after night for a period of about three months after his father's sudden death, when in dreams and hallucinations he followed the putrefaction of his father's corpse underground, then its luminous rejuvenation. Girodias tells me that strangely he has in recent times lived through a similar experience. He underwent a serious surgical procedure not long ago and prior to the operation was given a massive dose of sodium pentothal administered to him by an anaesthesiologist friend of his. For five days after his return from the hospital he felt utterly stoned, he says, adrift in a twilight state of consciousness, experiencing a recurrent dream in which he felt as if he had been buried alive in the earth and could taste the delicious dirt. This was tasting and savouring not in a merely physical sense but at some higher power of experience, an acute sensation of the mind and all the senses of delicious dissolution under the ground, as if one had been buried in a chocolate layer cake. The experience had prompted him to reflect that if this condition resembled the immediate posthumous state, if this were death, then it was not to be dreaded but desired.

Girodias insists on paying for our drinks. He has a polished Parisian manner of summoning a waiter which I cannot but admire. He is assertive, authoritative yet formally courteous. We leave Le Bonaparte together and part outside in the spring sunlight, shaking hands and wishing each other well.

One month after our meeting in Paris, I received a letter from Maurice urgently asking a favour of me. "I need a good English version of my newest publishing project," he wrote, "I thought of you as a potential saviour." He enclosed a French text, 17 pages in length, a typed prospectus for a publishing venture called Zoë, which was one of the projects he had mentioned during our conversation at Le Bonaparte. I must admit that I felt gratified and flattered (as perhaps he knew I would) that Girodias thought my command of French adequate to the task. And, hopeless romantic that I am, I relished the notion of working for the notorious Maurice Girodias. I knew, of course, that there would be no payment, though Maurice promised "eternal gratitude" and pledged to reward me "in some suitable way one day soon." My only recompense would be purely personal; I would gain deeper insight into Girodias' latest scheme and it would be an interesting task for me to undertake.

Girodias envisioned that the individual volumes of the Zoë series of books that he was offering for consideration to prospective investors would collectively constitute "a projected portrait of the 21st century," a future history of humankind. Each book was to be written by an expert in a particular area of knowledge and would predict likely developments in that field in time to come. The topics to be addressed in the diverse studies would include the U.S.S.R., minority rights, politics, money, intelligence, beauty, ecology, drugs, psychology and the hand-gun. The project was ambitious and provocative, but also informed by an earnest idealism. Obviously, Girodias must have hoped that the project would yield him a livelihood at the very least. But I believe that he also saw in the Zoë enterprise a possibility for vindication and even for a kind of redemption. From the tone of the prospectus I take it to be true that Girodias sincerely hoped for a better world. He believed that a better world could be achieved and he believed that books of the nature that he proposed to publish might serve in their way to precipitate the advent of such a world.

Unfortunately for Girodias and for a better world, nothing came of the Zoë project. As so often, he could not secure the necessary capital to launch the series, though as late as 1990 he wrote to me that he was attempting to salvage a part of the project by entering into discussions with Antoine Waechter, the head of the Ecology movement in France, with the aim of initiating a monthly magazine to be titled *Ecoregions,* supplemented by a collection of short books and pamphlets. In April of 1990,

Girodias wrote to me that in recent months he had been "going through the trauma of childbirth" in completing at last the second volume of his memoirs covering the years 1942 to 1962. The book was soon to be published. And he was already engaged in writing the third volume which would cover the time from his "flight to America" in the mid 1960s, "to my actual death as I anticipate it to happen, to appear in principle at the end of '90." Just above this sentence in smaller hand writing Girodias added: "the book not the death."

Published in the spring of 1990, *L'Arrivée,* the second volume of the projected three-volume autobiography, was well reviewed and sales of the book were brisk. Girodias began at last to receive something of the attention and admiration he had been lacking through long years of poverty and obscurity. Only a few months later, in early July of that year, while taping a radio interview, Girodias died of a heart attack. And so in an instant all plans were obviated, all goals cancelled, all projects ended. Except perhaps for one, the one in which in his inmost mind he had always believed: the journey of the spirit.

An Audience with the Emperor of Midnight:
Late night chats with Edouard Roditi

The other guests in the house retired at sensible hours, but like my host I was by nature a night owl and so we talked together and drank red wine until the small hours of the morning. The house, a narrow, three

story brick building, was located at 71 rue d'Ecosse, a little side street in Dieppe, and my host was the poet and polyglot, Edouard Roditi (1910 – 1992). The other guests included my wife Birgit, Genevieve, a middle-aged French woman, and two young poets from London, David Miller (born in Australia) and David Menzies (born in Scotland). It was August 1982.

Emperor of Midnight is the title of one of Roditi's collections of poetry, published in 1974 but gathering together texts both contemporary and from as far back as 1927. Although the author never attempts to explain the title, I interpret it as being psychologically self-descriptive. As an increment of the measurement of time, midnight is curious and anomalous. It is an instant apart from all others, astride two realms, uniting them, yet separate from both. It is an *interdiurnum,* an instant between successive days, the boundary between the last second of one day and the first second of the next day, a border and a meeting place, an interstice.

The tensions and divisions implicit in midnight may be seen to be reflected in the life and writing of Edouard Roditi, who occupied a curious and anomalous position in American letters, a position apart from all others.

Roditi was a surrealist and a modernist-formalist poet, a scholar, a critic (of art and literature), a philosophical anarchist and a student of mystical traditions, the author of love poems, political poems and devotional poems. He was an outsider with an Oxford classical education (Latin and Greek), a "security risk" in the U.S. and France, an admirer of both T.S. Eliot and Antonin Artaud. He was fluent in several languages other than English, including French, German, Spanish, Dutch, Turkish, Italian, Portugese and Hebrew. In at least three of these languages, Roditi wrote poetry, while from the others he translated both poetry and literary fiction.

In his personal life, too, there were complexities of identity. Roditi was an American citizen who was born in Paris and spent most of his life in France, he was of Sephardic Jewish descent, his sexual orientation was predominantly homosexual, and he suffered from epilepsy. Out of these disparate psychic provinces he shaped his own hybrid, midnight realm, a meeting place of words and worlds, styles and ideas, a sanctuary for antitheses, a personal poetic empire encompassing inspiration and control, the classical and the romantic, pessimism and despair and faith and hope.

Having spent a somewhat solitary boyhood in Paris, at the age of nine Roditi was sent by his parents to be educated in England, at Elstree School in Hertfordshire. The experience was, he said, deeply shocking. He was dismayed by the cold, unheated school and by the barbarous brutality of his classmates. It was here, however, that he had a fortuitous and memorable encounter with one of the most eminent authors of English literature, Joseph Conrad. The meeting with Conrad came about when the distinguished author was visiting the school to call on his old friend, the Head Master of Elstree. Roditi was enlisted to keep Conrad company while the Head Master tended to some pressing business. The agéd author and the lonely boy walked the school grounds speaking together in French since it gave Conrad (a polyglot like Roditi) pleasure to practice his fluency in that language. The matters of which they spoke were merely commonplace, Roditi said, Conrad questioning him about his studies and interests and relating in turn anecdotes from his own youth. But upon the occasion of their second and last meeting, Conrad suggested to the young Roditi that he might grow up to write in languages not his mother tongue, a strangely prescient prediction. More than six decades later, Roditi still remembered Conrad as a kindly, somewhat tired, old gentleman who spoke French with a slight accent.

Some nine years later, in 1928, at the age of eighteen, Roditi published his first poems in the celebrated Paris-based avant-garde magazine, *transition*. Writing poems both in French and in English, his method of composition was at that time that of the psychic automatism of the surrealists. During this same period, Roditi was studying at Oxford University where he wrote the first English and American surrealist manifesto, titled "The New Reality" which appeared in *The Oxford Outlook*. After only a few years, however, he abandoned the surrealist ethos and began writing poetry in a more formal fashion, organizing his verse in more traditional metrical and stanzaic structures. These poems appeared in mainstream modernist literary journals such as *The New Criterion* and *Poetry*.

Roditi related the story of his separation from surrealism in a document titled *The Journal of an Apprentice Cabbalist: Prelude to a Vita Nuova*, written in 1931 but first published in 1991. This account records how the poet's allegiance moved from Bretonian orthodox surrealism with its essentially materialist premises, toward neo-Platonism and the occult tradition, and the teachings of the Cabbala in particular. Yet, there is a sense in which Roditi may be seen not to have abandoned surrealism altogether but rather to have become two poets: one in the modernist manner and another as an independent, dissident, non-doctrinaire surrealist. The former tendency can be seen in collections such as his volume *Poems 1928-1948* and *Thrice Chosen* (1981), while the latter tendency is manifest in collections such as *New Hieroglyphic Tales* (1968), *Emperor of Midnight* (1974) and *Choose Your Own World* (1992).

In 1982, at the time of our visit, Edouard Roditi was a senior figure in American letters, a living link to the expatriate writers of the between-the-wars period. His work was published by New Directions and Black Sparrow, and appeared in literary journals as dissimilar as *Poetry, The Partisan Review, Kayak* and *Antaeus.* He had also very generously contributed poems and pieces to *Pearl,* a modest little literary magazine put out by Birgit and me in Denmark. We had corresponded and accepted his invitation to visit him at his house in Dieppe, travelling by train from Copenhagen to Paris and then to Dieppe, arriving in time for afternoon tea and a discussion among David Miller, David Menzies and Roditi on the merits of *Finnegans Wake.* "Joyce's knowledge of philology," Roditi said, "may have been sufficient to impress Gertrude Stein and Ernest Hemingway, but would never have passed muster at a good university." I was somewhat taken aback by this disparaging pronouncement but was soon to discover that Roditi held many such dismissive opinions. In literature, there were those writers whom he admired and whose work he championed and those he thought inferior, over-rated or merely wrong-headed.

At age 72, Roditi was thin-limbed with a protuberant belly. Behind large bifocal eyeglasses his eyes were hazel, sad and sensitive. His black hair (graying and thinning) was combed straight back. He wore a thin black moustache and sported long gray sideburns. He chain-smoked fil-tered Gauloise cigarettes and spoke with an R.P. accent (incongruous in an American citizen, of course, but he had learned to speak English orig-inally from his English mother and at the schools he had attended in Eng-land.) He had an endearing habit (probably acquired in England) of mak-ing some humorous observation and then, as if with a start, widening his eyes, raising his eyebrows and dropping his jaw in mock astonishment and saying: "Wot? Wot? " This charming mannerism was like something out of a Wodehouse novel. One late night, for example, we were discuss-ing the messianic megalomania of André Breton, when Roditi comment-ed: "He must have thought he was Joan of Arc in drag." He paused for a second, then looking at me with an expression of sudden surprise he pro-duced that face of amazement exclaiming: "Wot? Wot?" On another oc-casion, we were talking about the 19th century British painter, Richard Dadd, who killed his own father. Roditi observed: "Richard *Dadd*! Per-fect surname for a parricide!" (Look of stylized incredulity.) "Wot? Wot?"

Roditi was a gracious host and an accomplished cook. Every after-noon he would shop for the evening meal, shuffling resolutely through the crowded streets of Dieppe with a basket on his arm to a market on the square of the Eglise Saint-Jacque and then to a fish market on the Quai Henri IV. He prepared delicious vegetable soups, fried potatoes, fish filets and salads, served with white wine and followed by cheese and tea, and simpler meals of scrambled eggs, ratatouille, bread and Normandy cider. Talk at the table was often literary: Djuna Barnes he admired, Mina Loy and H.D. much less so, Cid Corman and other contemporary "open form" poets he esteemed very little, Ezra Pound not at all (deploring his influ-ence together with that of William Carlos Williams, "poor Bill" as he called him, upon younger poets) Allen Ginsberg occasionally, John Ash-bery frequently, Randall Jarrell, Stephen Stepanchev, John Haines and Kenneth Rexroth absolutely, T.S. Eliot unreservedly.

Of his old friend, Paul Bowles, Roditi said: "he is a very unhappy man," withdrawn and afraid of the world, only venturing out by chauffeured car to the post office and to purchase his supply of kif. He thought that Bowles, though he pretended to a "purely phenomenological interest" in things disturbing and unpleasant, was "obsessively fascinated by what horrified him." In this regard, Roditi found his friend's attraction to the bloody and sometimes violent ceremonies of Moroccan trance cults to be "morbid and masochistic."

Jane Bowles, too, Roditi remarked, had been unconsciously self-destructive. When he had first become acquainted with her in New York City in the 1940s Jane Bowles had been charmingly playful, buoyant and droll, but in her later years living in Tangier, she had become anxiety-ridden and desperately alcoholic. Beneath her puckish wit and eccentricity, Roditi believed, she had always been fearful of insanity, and in Tangier she had – much to her detriment – pursued a psychologically masochistic relationship with a malevolent Moroccan woman named Charifa, who may have poisoned her. There was a sense, Roditi said, in which Paul and Jane Bowles, both of them dear friends of his and both fine writers, were drawn together by a dark affinity. Driven by their respective obsessions, both had courted disaster in their lives.

We talked of dreams and Roditi said that during a period in which he underwent psychoanalysis he had kept a dream diary but the psychoanalyst had retained it. Imagery drawn from his dreams had been employed by him in several poems and in the collection of prose pieces titled *New Hieroglyphic Tales.* He was quite comfortable in speaking openly of his homosexuality, recounting with amusement how in his F.B.I. file there had been a letter describing him as a great womanizer when in fact at that time he had been "exclusively homosexual for 20 years."

Often at meals, out of respect for Genevieve, we conversed in French. Genevieve was, he told me, his "closest and dearest friend," though in truth, he said, they "hadn't much in common." She was interested neither in literature nor art, but he admired her greatly for being "unpretentious."

The hour late, the house quiet. Drinking red wine by lamplight. Roditi smoking cigarette after cigarette, wheezing, snorting and coughing. He smoked in this way, he explained, because he believed that tobacco helped to keep at bay the dreaded epileptic seizures to which he was subject. This affliction had since childhood occasioned him much distress, increasing his sense of isolation in the world. Yet often the seizures were preceded by a period of exaltation and enhanced mental capacities, during which he wrote poetry with great speed and fluency. Inevitably, however, after a time this euphoria turned to acute anxiety and physical anguish and ultimately to loss of consciousness followed by amnesia and a sense of complete depersonalization. During this latter phase, he inhabited for a time a spectral twilight state, a strange gray zone in which "one neither exists nor does not exist."

I remarked to Roditi how much I admired the elegy to Lorca he had written (part I of "Three Laments"). He thanked me and said that the poem had been deeply felt by him because he had known Lorca. They had been introduced through a mutual friend sometime in the late 1920s when Lorca was en route to New York via Paris. Roditi, a very young man at the time and still naïve concerning homosexuality, had immediately felt a deep affinity with Lorca and an intense attraction to him. They had shared a single night of love and then never met again. Some years later Roditi had with great sorrow read in a newspaper of Lorca's death. The memory of their one-night affair was even now very precious to him, the affinity between them had been strong.

Another poet, for whom he had felt a special bond of affection – though not sexual attraction – was Dylan Thomas. Roditi had first become acquainted with Thomas in London in the late 1930s and had spent many nights with him in Soho Pubs. He had last seen him just after the war and had one last pub crawl with him. Thomas' raucous, reckless behaviour was, Roditi thought, a compensation for sensitivity and self-consciousness, and for his status as a provincial Welsh outsider in the sophisticated, cosmopolitan London literary milieu. As one who as a Jew and a homosexual also felt himself an outsider, Roditi felt that there was between himself and Dylan Thomas an unspoken but mutually sensed, tacitly acknowledged kinship, a bond of respect and genuine fondness.

I mentioned having once read about his misadventures with Hart Crane. Yes, he said, what a débacle that evening had been. Roditi had quite unexpectedly one evening encountered Crane (whose poetry he revered) through a friend and had been dragooned into guiding his idol to a notorious bar in the depths of the 11th arrondissement. Crane was drunk and dishevelled, obstreperous and belligerent. Together they had travelled across Paris, negotiating dark tenement streets and finally arrived at the bar. Almost immediately, Crane had provoked an altercation with some French sailors and Roditi – fleeing for his own safety—had abandoned him there. For the young Roditi, not yet twenty years of age, the experience was memorably unsettling, a first-hand glimpse of a *poète maudit* in headlong pursuit of his own doom.

In all respects the direct opposite of Hart Crane, Roditi said, was T.S. Eliot, whom Roditi had met in London. Eliot was punctilious, polished, elegant and courteous. He was a person of absolute decorum but far from being aloof, he was genuinely gracious, genuinely kind. Eliot's careful dress and cultivated manners were, Roditi believed, a kind of protective coloration, safeguarding an essential shyness and self-consciousness in the man. Eliot had very generously encouraged Roditi in his writing, made incisive emendations to drafts of his poems, and had selected some of his poems for publication in *The New Criterion*. Roditi regarded Eliot as being in every sense "a saintly man" and unequivocally the foremost English-language poet of the century.

Among his contemporaries in American poetry, Roditi said, he had felt the closest personal, poetic and political rapport with the recently deceased Kenneth Rexroth. They had shared anarchist-pacifist ideals, held each other's work in high regard and found each other's company congenial. When they had last seen each other, Rexroth, already weak with ill-health, gazing at him with mournful eyes, had said: "Edouard, I wish I had been a homosexual so that we could have been lovers." Roditi had taken his hand and said: "That's alright, Kenneth, never mind. Actually, you're not my type."

We agreed that among Rexroth's best work were his translations from Chinese and Japanese poetry. Translation, Roditi said, was an art. (He had undertaken numerous literary translations from French, Spanish, Turkish, Dutch, German and other languages.) Satisfactory literary translation required many skills. You must, of course, have a very thorough grounding in the language from which you were translating, be familiar with the idioms, the weight of words, and most crucially you must be able to discern through the written words the individuality of the writer, that writer's distinctive voice. It was essential that you understand the subtleties and complexities of the text in its source language before presuming to render it in another language. You must also – and this was, he said, where so many translators were deficient – possess literary ability in your mother tongue.

What you aimed to achieve in a literary translation was to create something equivalent, something analogous not only to the original text, but to the perception or emotion that had inspired the text. In translating, you were through the exercise of your own creative resources seeking to transfer thoughts and emotions from one medium to another, one mind to another, without transforming or deforming them. That, he said, was translation as it should be practiced.

I mentioned Charles Henri Ford (among my own favorite poets) to Roditi, knowing that they had both appeared in *transition* at a very young age. "Oh, that Charles Henri," Roditi said with exasperation, "he's so *feminine!* He's *such* a fairy! His sister Ruth even refers to him as *my sister Charles Henri."* Roditi went on to relate how when they lived in Paris and Tangier in the 1930s, Charles Henri Ford had had a preposterous, unfathomable affair with Djuna Barnes, even typing for her the manuscript to her novel, *Nightwood. Nightwood* was brilliant, of course, but Djuna Barnes was a very strange person. She had once said: "I'm not a lesbian, I just loved Thelma Wood." And now she had become a complete recluse, refusing to see anyone, never venturing out of her apartment since sometime before World War II. He had learned from a friend in New York City that a cleaning woman for the apartments where Djuna Barnes lived had carried out boxes upon boxes of empty bottles from her flat, week after week. Apparently, she'd been drunk for decades!

Roditi paused and chuckled ruefully. "What a mine of bitchy stories I am!" he said.

Roditi was exceedingly well-read in the literatures of half-a-dozen languages and inclined to promote forgotten and neglected writers. Among those whose writings in English and American literature he thought worthy of re-consideration were Edward Bellowes, Horace Walpole, James Thomson, Philip Freneau, Artemus Ward, Sherry Mangan and Robert McAlmon. He valued original and eccentric writing and prized those flashes of vision sometimes to be found in the work of lesser literary lights. In Bellowes' verse he appreciated the poet's deployment of elaborate conceits and rhetorical extravagances that bordered on the hallucinatory. He thought Walpole's unremembered *Hieroglyphic Tales,* originally printed in an edition of only seven copies in 1785, were extraordinary and a clear precursor of surrealism. (Walpole's book served as an inspiration for Roditi's own *New Hieroglyphic Tales* published in

1968.) In James Thomson's *The City of Dreadful Night* (1880), he saw the expression of an ontological revolt as uncompromising and comprehensive as that expressed more than half-a-century later in the writings of Antonin Artaud. Philip Freneau he honoured for his Democratic revolutionary fervour, his broad human sympathies, his verbal harmonies and visionary nocturnal-gothic passages, the latter especially to be found in Freneau's long poem, "The House of Night" (1779). Roditi also commended to me the 19th century American humourists, Artemus Ward and Petroleum Vesuvius Nasby, whom he considered neglected "masters of the Absurd."

His own late near-contemporaries, Sherry Mangan and Robert McAlmon, he considered to have been undeservedly ignored in their time and now long forgotten. Mangan's poetry and writings were scattered among dozens of little magazines and remained uncollected. Probably Mangan's later Trotskyist zeal had contributed to his neglect as a writer. His work had, in any case, sunk without a trace. McAlmon's novel *Village* and his short-story collection *Distinguished Air* were very much worth seeking out. In person, Roditi said, McAlmon had frequently made himself unpopular among other writers for his waspish tongue and caustic wit. Cruel caricatures of several "Lost Generation" expatriate figures were to be found in his fiction.

An interesting link between McAlmon and Djuna Barnes, he said, was that both writers had used Dan Mahoney – a flamboyant, unsavoury, insufferable Irish-American expatriate, a transvestite queen – as a model for characters in their fiction. Mahoney was, of course, the model for Dr. Matthew O'Connor in Barnes' *Nightwood,* and he was also the inspiration for a short story by McAlmon. Mahoney was infamous in the Paris of the twenties and thirties, Roditi said, an abortionist, a quack, a cad, outrageously camp, endlessly garrulous, a master of malign wit, a brilliant bore.

Among living writers, Roditi very much esteemed Ned Rorem, a distinguished composer and the author of *The Paris Diaries* and *The New York Diaries.* Roditi urged me to read these books, even going to his bookshelf to find his copies and press them upon me.

I thought that Roditi's championing of forgotten and neglected writers was, perhaps, unconsciously motivated by his own sense that his work had for so long been ignored and underestimated. He complained that critics and anthologists in the United States thought he was French.

During the afternoons, Roditi was engaged in writing his "confessions," as he called them. The tentative title he had given to the manuscript he was typing was "Confessions of an American Epileptic." He gave me the early chapters to read. They dealt with his childhood and the pain and shame, the distress and loneliness his epilepsy had occasioned him then. He told me that he intended to write very frankly and explicitly concerning his homosexual experiences. He thought that James Laughlin (of New Directions) would likely be "too priggish, too cautious" to publish the book. He also showed me his most recent poem. (I forget the title.) It consisted of two end-rhymed quatrains on the subject of the house in which we were staying. He said that fifty years ago he could never have guessed that one day he would be writing in the manner of A. E. Housman. This thought caused him to roar with laughter.

Copenhagen (where Birgit and I lived) he loved, he said, for its "unceremonious hospitality." The Tivoli Gardens he thought delightful not least for their preservation of Commedia dell'Arte performances in the Pantomime Theater there. He enjoyed Danish food (smørrebrød, fresh fish) and the museums, including the Bertel Thorvaldsen Museum and the National Museum of Art. A Danish painter whose work he found compelling was Nicolai Abildgaard (1743-1809). Abildgaard combined neo-classical technique with a proto-romantic imagination to very impressive effect, he said. Particularly striking were Abildgaard's paintings illustrating Ludvig Holberg's curious satirical and surreal novel, *The Journey of Niels Klim to the World Underground (1741)*. This book which Roditi had read in a French translation he pronounced to be a classic of its kind and one strangely and unjustly disregarded by readers and scholars.

I asked Roditi if there were critics whose writings he held in regard. He named Nicolas Calas and G. A. Borgese, both men skilful and original in their analyses. Kenneth Burke was remarkable, very complex, very subtle, very stimulating, if sometimes somewhat verbose. And there was also Jean Paulhan, "a very complicated man, fragile and shy, erudite." Roditi had once produced for *Mesures,* a literary journal edited by Jean Paulhan, translations of poems by Gerard Manley Hopkins. Roditi and Paulhan had had minute discussions of the Hopkins poems, scrutinizing them word by word. Paulhan had impressed him as a very serious, very meticulous critic with many insights.

What he valued in criticism, Roditi said, was much the same as what he valued in poetry: individual intelligence and taste and culture applied to shared human experiences in the world. He deplored, he said, the retreat of poetry and much academic criticism into private worlds, private myths, private languages. This was essentially elitist, he thought, and current critical and poetic preferences for what was termed "pure poetry" had unfairly denied a place to and removed from consideration many other traditional genres of poetry, including satirical poems, didactic poems, topical, philosophical and even political poems.

In a similar manner, he said, he objected to the undue emphasis placed on technique in modern poetry. This was the basis for his complaint against the current generation of "open form" poets, whose poems seemed to him to have collapsed into solipsism. Technique should not be an end itself but should serve content, a content accessible to a reading public.

Perhaps because the hour was late and the darkness of the night out-side was at its darkest, I mentioned that his earlier descriptions of the twilight state that followed his epileptic seizures had reminded me of lines in Eliot's "The Hollow Men," in which an attenuated existence in the afterlife is imaged as "death's dream kingdom," and as a "twilight kingdom." I asked Roditi if he thought that the state of consciousness after death would be something similar to that strange condition he had experienced. He laughed and shook his head. "I'm no prophet," he said. Then he added: "But perhaps. Perhaps so."

We said our goodbyes on the night before our departure and Birgit and I left quietly early the next morning. We stole down the stairs and out the front door into the light of a late summer morning, leaving behind us still abed and adream the Emperor of Midnight.

Passing through:
Allen Ginsberg & Peter Orlovsky in Copenhagen, January 1983

As part of their reading tour through a dozen European countries, poets Allen Ginsberg and Peter Orlovsky, and their musical accompanist Steven Taylor, arrive by train in Copenhagen in the chill dark of an afternoon in early January of 1983. Birgit and I welcome them with red tulips and after shaking hands help them to carry their baggage from the platform upstairs and through the station to a taxi.

Allen is hatless, bespectacled and balding in a coat and muffler. Beneath his coat he wears a tweed jacket and sports a flowered necktie. His forehead is furrowed, his graying beard neatly trimmed, his right eyelid and lip drooping with a palsy with which he had lately been afflicted. Peter – despite the winter cold – is dressed in a yellow t-shirt emblazoned with the Naropa Institute logo and light cotton trousers. His feet are bare in a pair of flip-flops, his abundant graying light-brown hair worn in a long ponytail. His arms are muscular, his belly prominent. Allen says that they have come up in the train from Holland, haven't slept, and are very tired. They are going to be interviewed by a reporter from the Danish newspaper *Politiken* at their hotel and then in only a few hours hold their scheduled reading.

Peter walks the platform in a curious, crouching fashion, grimacing, groaning, grunting, but in a hoarse voice he courteously inquires as to where I am from and what I do. We struggle together up the stairs to the main floor of the station bearing between us a large and very heavy cylindrical cloth bag. When we reach the top of the stairs, Peter suddenly lifts the bag in one hand and to my astonishment and that of onlookers, he begins to spin with it, whirling, twirling, turning around and around across the floor of the railway station. From the outset, there is something in Peter's manner and behaviour that calls to mind the figure of Kaspar Hauser, an innocent abroad in a harsh and sordid world.

The reading is scheduled to be held in Huset (The House), a hip cultural center established in a former factory. A venue for music, theatre and other performances, Huset also contains a natural foods restaurant and a cinema. This evening there is an unforeseen problem. Shortly after Birgit and I arrive to claim our tickets and gain admittance to the reading, the entrance to Huset is blockaded by members of the Youth Club Personnel Union in protest at some grievance. The picket line (a solid phalanx of young people) is physically denying entrance to Huset to any and all patrons. (This despite the fact that the personnel who work in Huset have voted not to support the strike.)

When I catch sight of Peter, Allen and Steven in a hallway of Huset, I apprise them of the situation. Allen is thoughtful, not wishing to violate a picket line but not wishing either to disappoint those patrons who have come to hear them perform. We ascend together in an elevator to the room where the reading is to be held, a café with a small raised wooden stage. As Allen enters the room, there is applause from the approximately fifty guests who (like Birgit and me) arrived before the picket line was established. Before Allen can speak, though, a tall, thin young man with a sparse, scraggly beard and a shaven skull stands directly in front of him, raises his arm in a Nazi salute and shouts: "Heil Hitler!" Allen calmly ignores him and addresses the audience. "There is the question of the picket line to be considered," he says. He offers to go down to the entrance, attempt to reason with the pickets, and failing to persuade them to alter their course, he will deliver a brief reading for the congregation of about 150 aspiring, frustrated patrons who are waiting there in the winter cold. (Meanwhile, the madman continues to yell: "Heil Hitler!") The audience encourages Ginsberg to do this and he leaves the room.

Orlovsky remains, still dressed in his Naropa t-shirt, and now with a blue denim cap on his head. He paces barefooted and stiff-legged around the room, grunting and groaning. He dances on tiptoe, he approaches an elderly man seated at a table, shakes his hand and kisses it. He begins to brush his teeth, then brushes his long hair. He picks up a brass megaphone, balances it on one hand, holds it in his mouth by the handle, places it on his crotch like a giant erection, falls to the stage, pretending to writhe in ecstasy. He uses it as a telescope surveying the room, then employs it to amplify a series of animal noises: a dog barking, a rooster crowing. The audience cackles at these madcap antics. Peter kisses the wall, grows ever more passionate in his kisses, pats it, humps it. He lights a cigarette, resumes brushing his teeth, takes a swig from a bottle of Carlsberg. He then begins to wipe the stage curtains with a paper tissue. Meanwhile, Steven Taylor, a bespectacled, sensitive and intelligent looking young man, unpacks a guitar and begins to strum classical chords.

At length, Allen returns to the stage, explaining that everyone, including the pickets, has been invited up to the reading, but the pickets have not accepted that solution, so there's no more to be done. He unpacks his portable, hand-pumped harmonium and begins to chant in a baritone voice: Aaaaaaaahhhhhhhhhhhh. The chant rises and falls in the room, expressive of an infinite sorrow, an infinite longing for solace and refuge. He is joined in his chant by a suddenly serious Peter Orlovsky and by Steven Taylor who plays guitar chords behind the drone of the harmonium. The chant finished, Allen opens a black binder and reads "Birdbrain," a serio-comic poem condemning and lamenting the myriad manifestations of human selfishness and folly. The microphone is not working so he shouts the poem. The madman continues to shout at intervals and to applaud at incongruous moments. In response, Allen improvises lines in-

corporating the poor obnoxious man into the poem: "Birdbrain applauds
at the wrong time." He also alludes spontaneously to Peter now yodelling
alone somewhere in the distance beyond the room: "Birdbrain yodels in
the corridors of the Huset." And he mocks his own reading of the poem:
"Birdbrain keeps reading his poem no matter what interruptions there are."

Allen reads a poem on the death of his father, Louis Ginsberg, titled
"Don't Grow Old." He recounts how his aged, ailing father, reduced to
the state of an infant to be bathed, lifted and laid in bed by others, ruefully remarked to Peter: "don't grow old."

Allen also relates how he read poetry aloud to his dying father, including Wordsworth's "Ode: Intimations of Immortality." As he pronounced
to his father Wordworth's lines concerning how at birth the human soul
"cometh from afar / Not in entire forgetfulness / And not in utter naked-
ness, / But trailing clouds of glory do we come / From God, who is our
home, " his father sighed deeply and said to him: "That's beautiful, but it
isn't true." Now, harmonizing with Steven, Allen sings a melancholy
composition called "Father Death Blues."

At intervals, throughout the reading of poems and the singing, the
madman in the room continues to utter loud and enraptured "Heil Hit-
lers." Once, Ginsberg stops and with patient weariness addresses the
man, saying: "Please let me read. Please don't interrupt me. The poems
are quiet." There are further songs, "The Little Fish Devours the Big
Fish," and the lively "Do the Meditation Rock," and further poems, "The
Black Man," "What Are You Up to?" and "Libellous Poem." To all of
these, the Danish audience responds with much applause. During the
songs, Allen is accompanied by the delicate chords and rolling grooves of
Steven Taylor's guitar and accompanies himself on the portable red harmonium which he balances on his lap.

Then Peter, who has been smoking, staring and musing the while,
reads from his own collection of verse, the scandalously titled *Clean Ass-*

hole Poems & Smiling Vegetable Songs. Peter sits wide-legged on a chair, holding his book in his right hand, while with his left hand lifted in the air he gestures delicately, moving his fingers somewhat in the manner of a flamenco dancer. As Peter reads, Allen sits to one side of the stage, nodding approval, smiling, intent. Peter's poems include "First Poem," "Second Poem," "Dream, May 18, 1958," "Leper's Cry," "Someone Liked Me When I Was Twelve," and "Write It Down Allen Said." These are poems of buoyant whimsy, exuberant invention and deep seriousness. They are the poems of a guileless heart utterly bewildered by human cruelty and the world's deceit. Peter reads them with touching sincerity in his raspy voice. The audience reaction is enthusiastic.

There is an intermission, after which Stephen and Allen sing a country blues titled "When You Break Your Leg," and, joined by Peter, sing William Blake's "The Tyger," for which Allen has composed a melody. Then, Allen reads "America," (pausing occasionally in the course of his reading to explain to the audience certain allusions in the poem, such as references to the I.W.W., Tom Mooney, and the Scottsboro Boys, and improvising additional lines pertaining to current political events concerning President Reagan and Iran.)

The final poem of the evening is "Plutonian Ode." Alan stands, holding the recently published City Lights book of that title in his left hand, gesturing as he reads with his right hand, raising his right index finger like a teacher, closing his fingers in a fist, his body rocking, his shoulders shrugging, his hands trembling. (Orlovsky sits on a chair beside the stage, gaping enormous and protracted yawns.)

As Ginsberg begins part II of the poem, he drops the volume of his voice, reads calmly and tranquilly, then for the third and final section of the poem, builds force and volume, tension, drama, passion until the last syllable sound, resolving all in sorrow and affirmation: "Ah!" There is a gasp from the audience, then cheers and ardent and sustained applause.

The evening's performance ends with Allen and Steven singing Blake's "The Nurse's Song," while Peter yodels his accompaniment. The audience is exhorted to join in the refrain, "and all the hills echoéd." The audience is warm and gracious in its extended final round of applause.

The poems and the musical pieces are effectively paced and well-proportioned, complementary, rather like the balance between hymns and sermons in some church services. Indeed, the reading or performance taken as a whole bears some resemblance to a kind of ideological-cum-spiritual rite or ceremonial observance for the adversarial culture. A common denominator among the songs and poems performed is a summons to awareness, to resistance, to dedication.

The audience is encouraged to learn to meditate, to reflect on the brevity and vanity of life, to oppose the forces and agencies of injustice and oppression, and to practice the virtues of "patience and generosity" (as expressed, for example, in "Do the Meditation Rock.") For a poet considered by many to be avant-garde, irreverent and indecorous, Ginsberg seems in many ways closer to Vachel Lindsay and Carl Sandburg than to his hero Rimbaud or to his mentor William Carlos Williams. In his dramatic energy and his impassioned idealism echoes can also be heard of the populist prophets and militant labor orators of the American past. (I'm thinking of figures such as William Jennings Bryan and John L. Lewis, among others.) The physical voice in which Ginsberg brings his poems to life before the audience is familiar to me from tapes and records, a resonant baritone with east coast American inflections, his delivery richly cadenced, by turns conversational and incantatory. He is an expressive reader of his own poems, clearly aware that sound in poetry is integral to meaning.

Eleven days later we attend a second evening of readings and songs, held at Lyngby Storcenter, an American-style shopping center located in the town of Lyngby, north of Copenhagen. In the interim, Peter, Allen and

Steven have given a series of performances in towns and cities on the Jutland peninsula. Birgit and I arrive early and run into Allen at a snack bar. He says that he has just returned from a visit to Christiania (a self-proclaimed, self-governing "free town" within the city of Copenhagen, an abandoned military installation occupied in 1971 by slum-stormers, hippies and anarchists). The place reminded him, he says, of the slums of India. Allen looks spiffy, dressed for the evening's performance in a blue sports jacket, a white shirt, gray wool trousers, gray socks and scuffed black loafers. On the lapel of his sports jacket, he wears the gold pin of the American Institute and Academy of Arts and Letters.

At my request, he signs and inscribes my copy of *Plutonian Ode and Other Poems,* expressing his thanks for our having printed the title poem in our literary journal, *Pearl* (No. 6, 1978). Orlovsky joins us ordering a cup of coffee. We shake hands and he raises my hand to his lips, kissing it. His eyes are a clear blue. He is dressed as before in an orange Naropa Institute t-shirt, beads, bare legs in long blue shorts, bare feet in thongs, a blue denim cap atop his head.

As he drinks his coffee, he takes a pull on a small bottle of Danish schnapps he has bought. He asks me sincere questions about my job and my marriage. He tells me that he and his Spanish-speaking girlfriend will be having a child. When? I ask. In two years, he replies. He speaks to me of the farm where he lives, of the nuts and vegetables that he grows there, of the bees and goats that he tends. He says that he is not a good farmer, however, as he takes too much amphetamine. Peter signs my copy of *Clean Asshole Poems and Smiling Vegetable Songs.* He encourages me to meditate, a practice, he says, "invented by Lord Buddha 2,500 years ago," and recommends to me *The Jewel Ornament of Liberation* by Gampopa and Chogyam Trungpa's *The Myth of Freedom and the Way of Meditation.* These books are very valuable, very useful, very good, Peter says.

Fortunately, the Nazi madman does not attend the performance at Lyngby Storcenter. The reading takes place in an auditorium with a proscenium stage. The stage lighting is bright, harsh and hot. "We'll begin with music," Allen says to the audience and sings "Guru Blues" ("Father Guru") with Steven, while Peter sits nearby miming slyly and rubbing lotion on his feet. The next song is "Gospel Noble Truths," with the depressing refrain "die when you die," the rhyming text set incongruously but not incompatibly to a country and western tune. As Allen and Steven play their instruments and harmonize with their voices, Peter yodels in support.

Allen announces that Peter will read first tonight. Peter sits on a wooden chair, his legs spread wide, his bare feet flat on the floor. In a hoarse, whispering voice, enunciating carefully, holding a cigarette, he reads "America Give a Shit," "Write it Down Allen Said," (miming with his hands the images of "sub-machine guns" and "confusion") "My Mother Memory Poem," "Signature Changed," "4-D Man," and "Morris." The latter is a long and moving poem inspired by Peter's work as an orderly at Creedmoor State Mental Hospital in Queens, New York. The poem relates the story of a fleeting moment of human rapport achieved between Peter and a severely afflicted young patient. His reading ended, Peter places the palms of his hands together in prayer-like fashion and bows to the audience (the arjali mudra or namaste, more common these days but then rarely seen in the west.)

Allen tells the audience that he is going to read some of his early poems. From his copy of *Howl and Other Poems,* he reads "Sunflower Sutra," followed by a forceful, fervent rendering of "Howl," during which – now in shirtsleeves – he shouts and sobs, sweats and gestures. There is an intermission, and when Ginsberg returns to the stage he prefaces his performance by ringing his brass finger cymbals three times. Together with Steven and Peter, he sings "Prayer Blues" and "Airplane Blues," then reads "America" pausing after each line while his Danish translator, Erik Thygesen reads a translation of that same line. (All the while Peter clowns behind them, making faces, sticking out his tongue.)

"Father Death Blues" and "The Nurse's Song" follow, with "Tyger, Tyger" sung as an encore in response to prolonged applause from the audience. Before performing "Tyger, Tyger" Allen explains that he has composed the tune to Blake's poem to suggest the systole-diastole rhythm of the human heart: bum-búm, bum-búm, bum-búm.

He says that if, like Blake, we ask who made the wrath of war and bombs, if we ask who made the lamb, we must answer with and from our own hearts. After the reading is over, Ginsberg, looking depleted, hands me a piece of paper with the phone number of the Danish woman with whom they are staying in Copenhagen.

He tells me to phone at about 10 o'clock tomorrow morning.

On the following morning, I phone the number Allen has given me and we arrange to meet at the Swedish Embassy on Sankt Annæ Plads, where he and Peter and Steven are applying for permission to work in Sweden. At the embassy, Allen tells me that during their visit to Christiania Peter stepped on a piece of glass, cutting his foot, and should get a tetanus shot. Peter has also lost his eyeglasses somewhere and must get a new pair today since they are leaving for Sweden tomorrow. Allen would also like to visit the National Gallery of Denmark. He asks if I can help them on these errands. Of course, I can, I reply.

When they have received their temporary working permits, Allen consults a sheaf of papers he carries in the inside pocket of his coat. This includes their day by day schedule of readings. Satisfied that the Swedish working permits will cover the dates in question, we leave the embassy and hail a cab which I direct to an optometrist on Nørrevoldgade (not far from the City Hospital for Peter's foot and the National Gallery.) In the cab, Ginsberg mentions the translations of Sappho by Ed Sanders that I published in *Pearl*. We agree that they were very good. They compare very favorably, I tell him, with translations by Willis Barnstone and Mary Barnard, and with the "Poem of Jealousy" translation done by William Carlos Williams.

Ginsberg is familiar with these and adds that Sir Philip Sydney's translations of Sappho are interesting for having been written in Sapphics and Ezra Pound also had a go at writing in Sapphics in a poem titled "Apparuit." But it was the Sanders' translations that got him interested in the Sapphic verse form, Allen says. He says the form is complex and difficult to work with. The stanzas are composed of 4 lines each, consisting of trochees and dactyls. First three lines of two trochees, a dactyl, then two more trochees. Then comes the fourth line which is shorter, just one dactyl followed by a trochee.

As our taxi moves and stops in the streets of Copenhagen, Allen recites for me his poem, "Sapphics," as he does so counting the syllables and accents on his fingers.

At the optometrist, while Peter is tested and fitted for new glasses, Allen goes on to describe to me Ed Sanders' invention, the "Bardic Lyre." It's based, he says, on the ancient acoustic lyre, the four stringed tortoise shell lyre, but is a small, finger-operated electronic musical instrument intended to accompany recitations of poetry. Perhaps he will himself incorporate it into his own readings, Allen says. It might enhance the speaking of certain of his poems, the quieter, more lyrical poems.

We talk of the early experimental readings by San Francisco poets, Kenneth Rexroth, Kenneth Patchen and Jack Spicer, undertaken to jazz accompaniment, and Allen says how ungracious and ungenerous those same poets were, how catty, cranky and cantankerous they were about other poets. Rexroth, in particular, turned on so many of his friends, including ultimately Gary Snyder who was "the apple of his eye." Their falling out had occurred because Gary Snyder was appointed to some California cultural post and had generously, respectfully phoned Rexroth to offer him a grant. Rexroth had roared "You've sold out! I never want to talk to you again!" Then he had hung up. To Rexroth, Allen says, accepting any form of state employment or support meant selling out. I ask if Snyder and Rexroth were reconciled before Rexroth's death. Allen thinks they were not.

He goes on to speak of his own relationship with Rexroth. Once when drunk at Rexroth's apartment, in a moment of unwarranted indiscretion and youthful arrogance, Allen had said to his host: "I'm a better poet than you are, Rexroth." The next morning, mortified and remorseful, Allen had phoned to apologize but he had gotten the I-don't-ever-want-to-talk-to-you treatment. Rexroth had subsequently written a piece in which he expressed that in his estimation Ginsberg was "written out." And this had been before the publication of *Kaddish*. Allen thought that cultivating such spite and rancour was wrong. "A Boddhisatva should not act in this manner," Allen said, "should not aim for the heart, should not close off all chance of reconciliation." Rexroth had turned on Philip Whalen, too, and Jack Kerouac. After Kerouac had gotten drunk while visiting Rexroth and had supposedly frightened Rexroth's daughter – "I was there, he didn't do it" – Rexroth had written a vicious review of Kerouac's *Mexico City Blues*. In fact, Rexroth had compared the Beats to hoodlums, writing something to the effect that to come up against their work was like "going into a candy store for a pack of cigarettes and meeting a pack of juvenile delinquents." What had aroused Rexroth's unrelenting animosity, Allen said, was Robert Creeley's having an affair with Rexroth's wife, Martha, who was much younger than her husband. This had caused Rexroth to sour on the whole group. And he had never thereafter relinquished his vindictive attitude toward them. Allen recalled how many years later, he had called on Rexroth, bringing with him his agéd father, Louis Ginsberg. To Allen's relief, Rexroth had received them, but in the course of their polite conversation had cruelly asked Louis "how does it feel to have a son who's a better poet than you are?" This was petty, pointed revenge, Allen said, clearly directed at himself, but inflicted on an innocent by-stander. Louis had replied: "It feels marvellous."

Peter emerges from his eye test together with the optometrist who is grinning broadly and good naturedly at this unusual customer who seemingly has entertained him. While we wait for the prescription to be filled, Allen goes over their budget with Peter, producing from his pocket a detailed list of expenditures, discussing with him each item and outlay, including cab fare and new glasses, noting how much each owes to whom. Peter patently ignores him. "Don't you want to hear the information, Peter? " Ginsberg asks him. "Oh yes yes yes yes. Oh yes yes yes yes yes yes," Peter replies. "Mmmmm. Mmmmmm," he adds. To dispel the tension, both men light cigarettes. Allen says that he just started smoking cigarettes once again in Amsterdam after smoking some hash there. (Smoking hash in the European-style, that is mixed with ample amounts of tobacco.) He explains that they are on a tight budget, that's why they try to stay in the homes of local acquaintances or adherents rather than paying for hotels. Here in Copenhagen a woman named Lotte Thomsen has generously invited them to stay with her in her apartment, Allen says. "On the whore street," Peter adds. (Lotte Thomsen's apartment is located on Teglgaardstræde a short side street where aged, gray-haired, grandmotherly prostitutes display themselves in street-level windows.)

It is decided that we should have lunch. I offer to pay but they won't hear of it. "We have money," Allen says, "we're just cheap." Peter walks the winter sidewalks of the city in a stiff-legged hunch, blowing kisses to onlookers in bus windows, stopping to talk to an old lady, muttering "oh yes yes yes yes yes yes." I translate menus posted on the windows of cafés and restaurants and eventually we settle on a Chinese restaurant. During the meal, Peter eats voraciously, smacking, slurping, groaning, humming. At one point Allen tries to restrain him from eating more than his share. Peter lifts his plate from the table, and shovels the food piled on it into his mouth. When his plate is empty he raises it to his mouth with both hands and licks it clean with grunts of pleasure, then takes possession of the leftover rice, dowses it liberally with hot sauce and spoons it down, muttering "ummmm, ummmmm, very good, very good, very good." Allen regards him with a mixture of amused disapproval and fond indulgence, rather as a forbearing parent might regard a mischievous child.

As we eat our lunch, Allen asks me if I have read Tom Clark's *Poetry Wars.* (*The Great Naropa Poetry Wars,* published in 1980 recounts an incident that occurred during a Buddhist retreat under the direction of Ginsberg's guru, Chogyam Trungpa, where at the command of Trungpa the poets W.S Merwin and Dana Naone were seized in their rooms and forcibly and publicly stripped of their clothing.) Yes, I have read the book, I say. Allen says that although he was himself not present at the now notorious retreat, he has spoken with many who were present and has concluded that Tom Clark's account of the incident is "unrecognizably distorted." Clark, he says, has shown himself to be more than spiteful in this matter, indeed, "paranoid, psychotic." In Clark's book, Allen says, his statements regarding the parties concerned in the incident are quoted out of context. He had, in fact, said a number of good things about Merwin as a person and a poet, but Clark had perversely chosen to print only the negative remarks he had made. It was, of course, true that he had said that he would rather read Trungpa's poems than Merwin's. Indeed, he still finds Trungpa's poems "more interesting" than those of Merwin. But Clark's depiction of Trungpa surrounded by armed bodyguards was nothing more than "a paranoid fantasy." The misrepresentations disseminated by Clark had been harmful for the Naropa Institute which had found itself accused of "Buddhist fascism." And for attempting to defend Trungpa, Allen himself had been labelled a "Stalinist."

My offer to accompany Peter to the hospital while Steven and Allen go the National Gallery is accepted. In the emergency room I translate information to the desk nurse and then sit waiting with Peter. I ask him if the cut on his foot hurts him. "No," he says, "it feels good. Pain is good medicine. It clears consciousness." He says that with practice, through meditation, you can learn to isolate the pain and diminish it, perceiving it as only a small part of your whole body and a small part of your total consciousness. From his trouser pocket he draws forth a book that he recommends to me. It is *The Life and Teaching of Naropa* by Herbert V. Guenther, published by Oxford University Press, 1963. I ask Peter if he still plays the banjo. He did until recently, he says, but in Amsterdam he got so angry that he smashed his banjo to pieces. He got angry at President Reagan. "Reagan wants to kill everybody," Peter says. Peter's foot is treated and he is given a tetanus booster. We rendezvous with the others at the National Gallery.

Allen is primarily interested in seeing the work of the Danish painter Nicolai Abildgaard (1743–1809). He has recently seen and admired some of Abildgaard's paintings in the city of Aarhus after giving a reading there. Allen says he is intrigued by the connection between Abildgaard and Henry Fuseli and through Fuseli to William Blake. Peter and Steven are now feeling tired and return to Lotte Thomsen's apartment for a nap. Allen and I view the museum's collection of Abildgaard paintings. I translate titles. Allen is unhurried, focused, engaged and attentive in regarding the paintings, amused by Abildgaard's allegorical painting "The Cultural History of Europe," in which the figure representing Culture sleeps while fierce battles rage all about. Abildgaard's canvases depicting Philoctetes, Anakreon, Sappho, and Ossian also draw his admiration. Another Danish painter singled out for praise by Ginsberg is L.A. Ring (1854–1933).

We pause before his melancholy painting titled "In the Churchyard of Fløng," which depicts an old woman with wrinkled countenance and faded blue eyes sitting with hands folded on her lap before a grave in a country churchyard. The dates of birth and death inscribed on the cross at which she stares indicate that the grave is that of her late husband. She sits beneath a leafless winter tree. The churchyard is set among barren fields. Far in the distance can be discerned the steeples of a church.

Allen comments upon her facial expression, the grief, the desolation and despair, the utter lack of hope and illusion. She is thinking, he says, back to her girlhood and the notions of life she held then and she is thinking forward to her own death. Life is not what she once thought it to be, he observes, life is death and it has always been so even when as a girl she thought otherwise. The church so small and insignificant in the misty distance can offer her no comfort or consolation. She is alone, he says, with her stark awareness of "the enormity and finality of death."

Allen is elated by the Emil Nolde paintings and delighted by the Rembrandts. He studies closely a Rembrandt portrait of an old lady and remarks upon the profound sorrow and disillusion expressed in her woebegone face, comparing it to that of the woman depicted in the painting by L.A. Ring. Discovering the museum's collection of paintings by Peter Bruegel the Elder, Ginsberg gasps with "oh" and "ah." He is particularly taken by the large Bruegel painting of "Christ Driving the Traders from the Temple," which he examines closely and at length. He remarks to me that "Bruegel is like Shakespeare in his poetic composition." Allen points to details in the painting, arguing that not only the money changers but nearly everyone in the crowd around the temple is engaged in some form of grasping greed, including the beggars, a thief, a quack doctor, and the many merchants and farmers who have come to buy or sell animal stock. And in the lower right hand corner of the painting there is a half-naked child aged about four years, facing out from the canvas with a look of terror in his eyes, innocent witness to this appalling human spectacle. (I think of Peter.)

We view paintings by Mantegna, Lucas Cranach the Elder, Titian, Rubens and others, discussing artists and paintings referred to in Pound's *Cantos,* then retire to the basement canteen for coffee. Allen tells me that he is contemplating writing an epic poem based upon a dream he had the previous night. In the dream, Allen recounts, he passes through a tunnel into a magic castle. This is a domain where wishes are fulfilled but where guru-tricks are also played upon those who enter. Here, he encounters a beautiful naked black man who asks him: "do you want me?" "Yes!" Allen replies avidly. "Look here," the black man says, indicating a diseased portion of his chest. "How are your other parts, your limbs?" Allen asks and is shown other disfigured and unwholesome areas of the man's otherwise alluring body. Later, a young boy offers himself to Allen but sud-denly vanishes. There the dream ended. Allen compares it to Keats' poem, "Christabel," which relates the encounter between Christabel and a mysterious, beguiling figure named Geraldine whose body is ultimately revealed as bearing some terrible disfigurement that mars "her bosom and half her side."

Allen also compares the dream to the "Magic Theatre" section in Her-man Hesse's novel, *Steppenwolf.* The "Magic Theatre" is a realm where fantasies – including erotic fantasies – can be lived out and where spiri-tual or psychological instruction takes place. The dream, Allen says, has lingered in his mind and absorbed his attention all day. Perhaps he can use it as the basis for a new poem, but he mustn't strive, he says, striving would create an anxiety that could drive away the meaning and inspira-tion offered by the dream. He adds that dreams have served him in other ways at other times. He has even composed lyrics in dreams. The first stanza and general outline of "Guru Blues," for example, were conceived in a dream.

Outside, early winter darkness has fallen. We take a bus through the city to the editorial offices of *Politiken,* a Danish newspaper that has promised him payment for an interview he gave to a reporter on the night of his arrival in Copenhagen. Unfortunately, it proves that the payment cannot yet be made to him, so Allen leaves a forwarding address where he will be staying while in Sweden. He is clearly disappointed, even be-coming testy with the young man at the reception desk. We walk the raw, evening streets of Copenhagen to Teglgaardstræde where Allen and Peter and Steven will be sleeping one last night before leaving tomorrow morn-ing for Sweden. In the light of the antique street lamps, his face looks drawn and weary. He seems a sad man. I think that the discourses he de-livered on the sorrowful, disillusioned faces of the old women in the paintings at the National Gallery were, in part, projections of his own current state of spirit. The preoccupation with his father's death and with "Father Death" in his recent poems and songs would seem to bear this out. And there would seem to be but little consolation to be drawn from the rather bleak Buddhism he embraces.

We ascend the wooden stairs of the old building where he is staying, walk a dim hallway, and enter an apartment with half-timbered walls. Peter is asleep. I shake hands and say goodbye to Steven and ask him to say goodbye to Peter for me. I shake hands with Allen who thanks me and says: "Well, we saw some Bruegels and Rembrandts together." We speak our final farewells and I descend the stairs into the dark, windy street. I leave them there to their lives in which this has been but one day, Allen and Peter, two ageing heart-friends whose fates and souls are so interwoven, both seeking salvation, both struggling still with vanity and anger, both alone, both far from home this winter night.

Bios Xenikon Blues [II]

It came upon me that not only could I no longer buy a hamburger or a taco or baloney or dill pickles or braunschweiger or peanut butter, but I could no longer buy a copy of *Harper's, The Atlantic, Esquire* or *The Saturday Review.* And, of course, as you would expect, in Danish bookshops and libraries nearly all of the books were in Danish. And there were other things to contend with: the monetary system, the metric system of weights and measures, the Celsius scale, the notation of months and days on letters and documents, the numbering scheme for a building's floors, together with light switches and door locks that operated in perverse ways. Nor to my frustration could I follow the news on the radio. It sounded to me like *zah-zah-zah-zah Nixon zah-zah-zah-zah Vietnam zah-zah-zah-zah.* I knew what they were talking about but I did not know what they were saying about it. As the writer, Nathaniel Parker Willis, once observed: "It's a queer feeling to find oneself a *foreigner.*"

After some months in Denmark, browsing at a newsagent one afternoon, I discovered the *International Herald Tribune* or the IHT as I later learned that it was affectionately called by its readers. I had never heard of this legendary paper, edited in Paris. In Ernest Hemingway's *The Sun Also Rises* (1926) the protagonist Jake Barnes reads it in a café while sipping a glass of wine. In Alfred Hitchcock's *The Lady Vanishes* (1938) the characters Charters and Caldicott vainly search the pages of the Paris *Herald Tribune* for the latest cricket scores. And perhaps most famously, in Jean-Luc Goddard's film *Breathless* (1960), the character played by Jean Seberg sells copies of the newspaper on the streets of Paris. The IHT printed the news, of course, but more importantly for my homesick heart it also had American comics and sports pages and a weather map and temperatures in the U.S. To help express the great pleasure occasioned me by the IHT – the sense it afforded me of contact and communion with home – let me quote Richard Henry Dana's *Two Years Before the Mast* (1840): "No one has ever been on distant voyages, and after long absence received a newspaper from home who cannot understand the delight that they give one. I read every part of them – the houses to let; things lost or stolen; auction sales and all. Nothing carries you so entirely to a place and makes you feel so perfectly at home, as a newspaper."

In 1972, the IHT in Denmark cost the equivalent of about 35 cents. How poignantly cheap that seems today, but at that time I had so little money that I bought the newspaper only very occasionally as a special treat. And, like Richard Henry Dana, I pored over it, reading everything (except the finance and business pages). I read all the various columns, including the gossip column, also, of course, the book review, the letters to the editor, even the Classified Advertisements including personnel wanted ("English speaking cook for the permanent delegation of the Sultanate of Oman to UNESCO"), situations wanted, real estate, ("Exceptional castle in Bruges"), religious services ("the American Church in Paris, St. Joseph's English Speaking Catholic Church"), business opportunities, announcements, matchmaking services, autos tax free, leisure and travel, and the personals. I only regretted that I couldn't follow the columns on chess and bridge, nor was I clever enough to work the crossword. I was unfailingly intrigued by the IHT logo. In the center was a clock with Roman numerals, the hands reading twelve minutes past six. Atop the clock an eagle was perched facing right. To the left of the clock was a seated figure of Father Time holding a scythe, brooding over an hourglass set before him. Beyond him, in the distance were pyramids and a caravan of camels and riders; there were tall pillars of a temple and nearer the foreground a man plowing with an ox. These I took to represent the past or the old world. To the right of the clock were representations of the new world, specifically the United States. Standing above a large industrial gear wheel was a woman in liberty cap holding an American flag; about and beyond her were sheaves of grain, the smoking chimneys of factories, telegraph or telephone poles, and a steam train crossing a bridge. The paper was established in 1887 so I believe that the logo was probably created at that time. At some point, during the postwar period, the steam train was re-drawn as a modern diesel train and a jet liner in flight was added to the illustration. I suppose that in both its versions the nameplate logo of the IHT was meant to express the link between the past and the present, the old world and the new, and perhaps also to suggest that the new world (i.e. the United States) was now at the forefront of history, its achievements superceding and surpassing those of ancient Egypt, Greece and Rome.

I enjoyed learning the temperatures high and low in Phoenix and other American cities for "today" and "tomorrow," (actually the IHT was often already a day or two old when I bought it at the newsagent). And I took pleasure in studying the weather map with its depiction of the jet stream moving across North America. I read with interest the scores and standings of college sports teams and professional sports teams across the United States. During the Major League Baseball season line scores were a particular pleasure. And, every spring at around opening day in the pages of the IHT there appeared a poem by Dick Roraback, the sports editor of the newspaper, titled "The Crack of a Bat" conveying the melancholy that afflicts Americans living abroad when the baseball season begins. In those days the comics included classics such as "Rip Kirby," "Beetle Bailey," "Pogo," "Buz Sawyer," "Rex Morgan," "Lil Abner," "Miss Peach," "Dennis the Menace," "Blondie," "Wizard of Id," "B.C." and "Peanuts." Among the personals in Classified Advertising there often appeared the very touching and inspirational prayer to the Sacred Heart of Jesus and Saint Jude, together with thanks from those who had experienced "miraculous help" after reciting the prayer. Long-established and a permanent feature in the pages of the IHT was the endearing advertisement for "Harry's New York Bar, Paris," located at 5 rue Daunou, with its slogan informing the prospective patron: "Just tell the taxi driver, *sank roo doe noo.* "

Decades after I first encountered the IHT, reading it in sickness and in health, reading it sitting in a chair at home, in hotel rooms in Paris and Hamburg, on buses and on trains, there opened in Copenhagen a café -- Café Europa – the owners of which subscribed to the IHT. Attached to a stick made of varnished blonde wood, the newspaper was made available to customers. It was an exquisite expat pleasure to taste rich bitter coffee while inhaling the fragrance of freshly printed ink from the crisp pages of the *International Herald Tribune.* Alas, some sleek CEO (may his name be forever lost between sofa cushions) put an end to the hallowed IHT. In contempt of history, tradition, distinction, character and charm, some once-born CEO clad in emasculated pants killed off the IHT with its venerable logo and its rich romantic past and in its place launched the insipid *New York Times International Edition* containing no U.S. weather, a scant handful of comics and depressingly meagre and infrequent coverage of American sports. No longer a newspaper for Americans abroad, the paper now seems aimed, instead, at a readership of jet-setting, Armani-suited, baseball-hating Asian businessmen who probably only buy it to read the business and finance pages.

Even as we look on, familiar things disappear from the world around us; eras come to an end. (One hundred and twenty-five years of the Paris *Herald Tribune* brought so abruptly to conclusion.) What has always engaged my attention is the way in which eras overlap and interpenetrate with one another and the way certain fugitive objects and persons from one era outlast their time, lingering and clinging to existence in the midst of another time. When I was growing up in Arizona in the 1950s, in an age of automobiles and television and jet airplanes, the last arthritic bandits and gunfighters of the late frontier era were passing away, their obituaries appearing in local newspapers. And still living then were old men who had served in the Spanish- American war or the Mexican Punitive Expedition or seen action in the last engagement between the U.S. Cavalry and Yaqui Indians in Bear Valley, Arizona in 1918. Sometimes, even in the late 1960s, you could still glimpse the fading contours of the territorial era in Arizona. I remember Parry's bar in Tempe where on Sunday afternoons the oldtimers sat at a round oak table playing pinochle. Indeed, at that time, Carl Hayden, who had been born in Tempe (then called Hayden's Ferry) in 1877 and who had served as horseback-riding sheriff of Maricopa County, running down train robbers in the territorial days, still held office in the United States Senate.

Living in Europe, separated from my home, I became increasingly fascinated with vestiges, remnants, residues and traces, with eras abating or subsiding, with dying echoes of former times, with scattered fragments of the past and sediments deposited by the river of time. It was in pursuit of this preoccupation that I sought out aging survivors of earlier literary eras, writers living – as it were – in the epilogue of their stories, and trawled flea markets and used bookshops for artifacts.

I have, indeed, spent a fair portion of my life in second hand bookshops. In the cluttered cellars and dim backrooms of such shops I have rummaged for whole afternoons through cardboard boxes and paper bags of old books, crouched to examine volume by volume piles of worn paperbacks and precarious stacks of scuffed and faded clothbound books, stood unsteadily atop ladders searching among the dusty tomes on top shelves, and knelt to reach beneath the bottom shelves (where spiders dwell) for books deposited and forgotten there long ago. I have sometimes thought that the process of delving down through strata of printed matter in the less accessible corners of second hand bookshops bears comparison to archaeological excavation. Occasionally from among all this detritus and debris of the printed word, from out of the agglomeration of lost, forgotten, homeless books that throng the shelves of thrift shops and the humbler sort of second hand book bookstore, I have retrieved the kinds of books that connect me to the romantic past or to momentous events of history.

The flotsam and jetsam of time and strife are often cast up at flea markets, at church bazaars, in junk shops, in charity shops and in used bookshops. Once, in the years immediately before I was born, a great tide of American soldiers and American material flooded into Europe. After the war ended, that tide withdrew, leaving behind it scattered debris, objects lost or discarded. I have found among the jumble of wares spread on tables and blankets at flea markets items of U.S. Army web gear – a metal canteen with cup and cover, the cover stamped "N.W.I.S. Union Made U.S. 1943," the cup stamped "U.S.E.A. Co. 1944," and an M-1 carbine canvas muzzle cover made by "Victory Mfg. Inc. 1944," – as well as a *Field Manual for the Identification of German Aircraft*, and shoulder patches for the 3rd Army and the 76th Division.

I am not a collector of militaria, but these artifacts touch me and intrigue me. What are the hidden histories of the objects we find and by what strange chain of chance were they brought into our hands? Manufactured upon a day long ago and in a land far away by human hands now long dead, shipped across the wartime Atlantic, used by young American soldiers now also these many years later gone from the light of day. Nineteen forty-three, nineteen forty-four, how extraordinary to reflect that those years were actually-existing, really-occurring years, each day a real day of time; and that those factory workers and soldiers and sailors were real persons, each mind aware, alive and real. These scattered objects I've salvaged were left behind here. Outliving their original makers and

owners, they have somehow survived though all the years, enduring mis-
prized and unremarked somewhere as history moved on. Seeing them,
holding them in your hands, you sense the strangeness of the past.

More fragile and more ephemeral artifacts of World War II are two
C-ration matchbooks that I found on separate occasions. The front cover
of one matchbook reads: "We must win! Buy more War Bonds, Stamps;"
and on the reverse side: "Our first duty. Buy more War Bonds, Stamps."
On the front cover of the other matchbook, there is a stark warning: "Easy
to Pick-up," while the reverse side depicts a Sad Sack type G.I. gazing
with enraptured fascination at a sexy young woman clad in a tight dress
with a high hemline and a low neckline. Above this illustration in bold
ragged font are printed the letters: "V.D."

Over the many years that I have lived here I have also found – in
Denmark, in Germany, in Belgium, in Holland and France – more than a
hundred copies of Armed Services Editions books. These are lightweight
paperbound books (four by five and three-quarters inches) designed to fit
into the pocket of a field jacket or a pea coat. They are printed on poor-
quality wartime pulp paper with double columns of print in a horizontal
format and bound by staples or with a glued spine. The books were distributed free-of-charge to servicemen and servicewomen in the various
theatres of war. The range of titles and genres is impressive. There are
books of poetry, mysteries, westerns, fantasy and science fiction, bestsell-
ers, classics, biography, philosophy, psychology, music, science, humor,
sports, and many other categories. I have read that there were 1,322 individual titles in the series and that the total number of printed volumes was
over 120 million. The majority of these, it is said, were consumed in use,
that is to say read to tatters during the war. The copies I have found of
these frail artifacts are often creased and worn and have clearly seen a bit
of life. Their decomposing pulp pages give off a scent like that of vanilla.
Touching these books I always wonder whose hands once held them,

whose eyes read the pages long ago and what may have been that reader's fate.

I like to think that I am rescuing them from loneliness and oblivion, these scattered scraps of the war, languishing forgotten and unloved in the back rooms of junk shops and used book shops. I exult to find in a box two pocket-size U.S. Army Language Guides, one for Danish and one for German. These booklets – printed in 1943, their staples now brown with rust – were intended to help U.S. soldiers communicate with the inhabitants of the countries they were liberating or invading. Useful words, phrases and simple sentences in the target language are written out phonetically to approximate native-speaker pronunciation. In the Danish phrase book there are sections covering greetings and courtesies, numbers, food, directions, but there are also phrases such as "Take cover!" "Where are the soldiers?" and "I am wounded." Phrases in the German language guide have a sharper edge to them: "Don't try any tricks," "Obey or I'll fire," "Throw down your arms," "Raise your hands." Odd and sad now to envision the human situations in which such words might once have been spoken, but a bleak reminder of life's rigid exigencies.

Other printed artefacts of World War II that turn up from time to time in my somewhat obsessive searches are Overseas Editions. These pocket-sized volumes (four and three-quarters by six and three-eighths inches) were for distribution among civilians in those countries liberated by Allied troops. They were intended to inform the citizens of those countries about America, its culture, its literature, its form of government and its vision of a postwar world. The covers of the books are uniform, a depiction of the Statue of Liberty and a statement reading: "This edition of an American book is made available in various countries only until normal free publishing, interrupted by Axis aggression can be re-established." Titles include *How America Lives* by J.C. Furnas, *U.S. Foreign Policy and U.S. War Aims* by Walter Lipmann, *TVA: Democracy on the March* by David E. Lilienthal, *On Native Grounds* by Alfred Kazin, *How New Will the Better World Be?* by Carl L. Becker, biographies of George Washington Carver and Benjamin Franklin, as well as novels such as *The Human Comedy* by William Saroyan and *For Whom the Bell Tolls* by Ernest Hemingway. How poignant it all seems today. These now yellowed pages imbued with wartime belief and hope, these optimistic, idealistic, light-at-the-end-of-the-tunnel books, scattered, forgotten, orphaned, forlorn.

More piquant by far than the above, though perhaps no less poignant in their way, are the risqué paperbound English-language books once printed in Paris for a readership of raffish English and American tourists and horny, homesick postwar G.I.s. Volumes from the Obelisk Press (interwar era) and the Olympia Press (postwar era), surface still at flea markets and are still occasionally to be found in dank cellar bookshops, stranded there with the ebb tide of changing cultural norms. Once contraband, these books are now mostly quaint, the exceptions being the still potent writings of Henry Miller, William S. Burroughs, J.P. Donleavy, Vladimir Nabokov and a few other authors. Though landmark decisions in the courts of the U.S. and the U.K. have long ago legalized literary pornography, I still savour the feeling of buying once forbidden books, experiencing the pleasantly nostalgic frisson of retrospective transgression.

Mainstays of my expat reading over the years have been paperback books from Tauchnitz Editions and the Albatross Press, both continental publishers of English-language literature. Already in 1842, Tauchnitz began publishing re-prints of English and American authors and continued to do so until its premises in Leipzig, Germany, were destroyed by an allied bombing raid in 1943. During this one hundred year run, approximately 5,400 individual volumes by nearly 800 authors appeared. Practically every English and American author of consequence – from Charles Dickens to Ernest Hemingway – was included in the Tauchnitz collection. The Albatross Press or The Albatross Modern Continental Library was an elegant, innovative latecomer to continental English-language publishing, founded in 1932 with editorial offices in Hamburg, Germany. Before they ceased operation with the declaration of war in September of 1939, they had printed nearly five hundred titles, including biographies, mysteries, adventure, travel and cutting-edge contemporary fiction. Both Tauchnitz and Albatross editions carry the printed warning: "Not to be introduced into the British Empire or the U.S.A." I feel fortunate to have fallen heir to this vital legacy, to the literary riches of these two publishers whose aging books, outlasting their era, are still to be found in used bookshops in Denmark and throughout Europe.

These artifacts I sought out and gathered about me for sustenance and shelter. I hoarded them as talismans. I cherished them as palpable links to the past, feeling through them a sense of kinship with their previous owners and readers and a sense of connection with the era in which they had originated. Time runs on. Eras end. Objects become dispersed. Things dissipate and disappear. I just wanted to see some of it, save some of it. Years pass in the pursuit and accumulation of artifacts and one day you realize that you have yourself become a kind of artifact, a relic from a bygone era. An old man in a foreign land.

Ornithologists speak of vagrant birds, also called accidentals. These are birds that have strayed from their customary breeding or migrating range. A bird is considered vagrant if it has come to rest in a completely foreign territory. Such birds may have been blown off course by storms. The ancient Greeks used the term "metoikos" to designate a resident alien, one who has changed his or her home, an outsider. The Welsh language contains the richly suggestive word "hiraeth," said to mean longing for a home you can't return to, a combination of homesickness, yearning and grief for what you have lost, an anguished sense of separation from home. A similarly layered and poetic word – "saudade" – is to be found in the Portuguese tongue. This word encompasses a sense of incompleteness, a melancholy nostalgia, a profound yearning to be near again to a beloved person or place that is lost or distant. In *Redburn* (1849), Herman Melville writes: "Oh, he who has never been afar, let him once go from home, to know what home is."

How often I have known a hollow far-from-home sorrow, a wild longing for home. You end by being neither there nor here. You neither live where you belong, nor belong where you live. Yet, from this uncoveted condition an insight may be gleaned. There is a sense in which all of us live our lives in exile, parted from the source and center of our being, severed from our true homeland. Seen in this way, we may all be said to be living *bios xenikon,* the life of a stranger, all of us resident aliens on this earth and in this life, all of us strangers and exiles.

Lightning Source UK Ltd.
Milton Keynes UK
UKHW02f1614310818
328095UK00006BA/36/P